NATIONAL GEOGRAPHIC
KiDS

BEGINNER'S
UNITED STATES
ATLAS

NATIONAL GEOGRAPHIC
WASHINGTON, D.C.

Table of Contents

What Is a Map?

An atlas is a collection of maps and pictures. A map is a drawing of a place as it looks from above. It is flat, and it is smaller than the place it shows. Learning to read a map can help you find where you are and where you want to go. **Mapping your home ...**

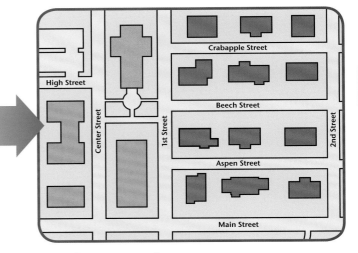

From a bird's-eye view ...
If you were a bird flying directly overhead, you would see only the tops of things. You wouldn't see walls, tree trunks, tires, or feet.

On a large-scale map ... you see places
from a bird's-eye view. But a map uses drawings called symbols to show things on the ground, such as houses or streets. The map of the National Mall in Washington, D.C., on pages 10–11 is an example of a large-scale map.

Finding places on the map

A **map** can help you get where you want to go. A map helps you read it by showing you north, south, east, and west, plus a key and a scale.

→ A **compass rose** helps you travel in the right direction. It tells you where north (N), south (S), east (E), and west (W) are on your map. Often only a north arrow is used.

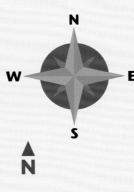

→ A **map key** helps you understand the symbols used by the mapmaker to show things like buildings, towns, or rivers on the map.

★ State capital
•• City or town
■ Point of interest
--- National trail
•••• Country boundary
······ State boundary
☐ Indian Reservation
☐ State Park
☐ National Park Service
☐ National Forest land

← A **scale** tells you about distance on a map. The scale shows what length on the map represents the labeled distance on the ground.

0 ——————— 100 miles
0 ——————— 100 kilometers

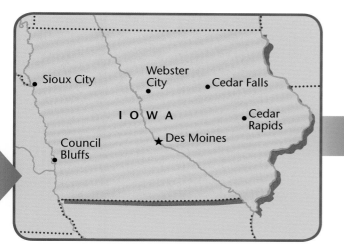

On an intermediate-scale map ...

you see a place from much higher up. A town appears as a tiny dot. You can't see houses, but you can see more of the land around the town. Most maps in this atlas show a whole state with its towns and other special features.

On a small-scale map ... you can see

much more of the country around a state, including other states. But on a small-scale map there is much less detail. You can no longer see most features within the state. Two states—Alaska and Hawai'i—are often shown in separate boxes or on a map of the whole continent, as on pages 6–7.

Map Key for the State Maps in This Atlas

- • Aspen ....*town of under 25,000 residents*
- • Frankfort ....*town of 25,000 to 99,999*
- • San Jose ....*city of 100,000 to 999,999*
- • New York ....*city of 1,000,000 and over*

⊛   National capital
★   State capital
⌒   Pass
▪   Point of interest
+   High point
·   Low point
────   River
────   Intermittent river
┼┼┼┼   Canal
▪▪▪▪▪   Bridge
─────   National trail
••••••   Country boundary
··········   State boundary
··········   Continental Divide
   Lake
   Intermittent lake

Dry lake
Swamp
Glacier
Sand
Lava
Area below sea level
Indian Reservation (I.R.)
State Park (S.P.)
National Park Service
National Historical Park (N.H.P.)
National Lakeshore
National Marine Sanctuary (N.M.S.)
National Monument (NAT. MON.)
National Park (N.P.)
National Preserve (N. PRES.)
National Recreation Area (N.R.A.)
National River
National Scenic Area
National Seashore
National Volcanic Monument
National Forest land
National Grassland (N.G.)

The Physical United States

The Land

 Land regions The rugged Sierra Nevada and Rocky Mountains run north to south through the western United States. Between these mountains are dry lands with little vegetation. East of the Rockies are wide, grassy plains and the older, lower Appalachian Mountains.

 Water The Mississippi–Missouri is the longest river system in the United States. The Great Lakes are the largest freshwater lakes in the country.

Climate The United States has many climate types—from cold Alaska to tropical Hawai'i, with milder climates in the other 48 states.

Plants The United States has forests where there is plenty of rain. Grasslands cover drier areas.

Animals There are many kinds of animals—everything from bears and deer to songbirds large and small.

← North America is famous for its **deciduous forests.** Leaves turn fiery colors each fall.

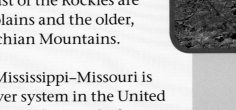

↑ Waves off the Pacific Ocean roll onto a beach along the shore of Moloka'i, one of the islands that make up the state of **Hawai'i.**

← The majestic bald eagle is the national bird of the United States. It is found throughout the country, but about half live in **Alaska.**

↓ Deserts are found in the southwestern part of the United States. This large rock formation, called the Mitten, is in **Monument Valley** in Utah.

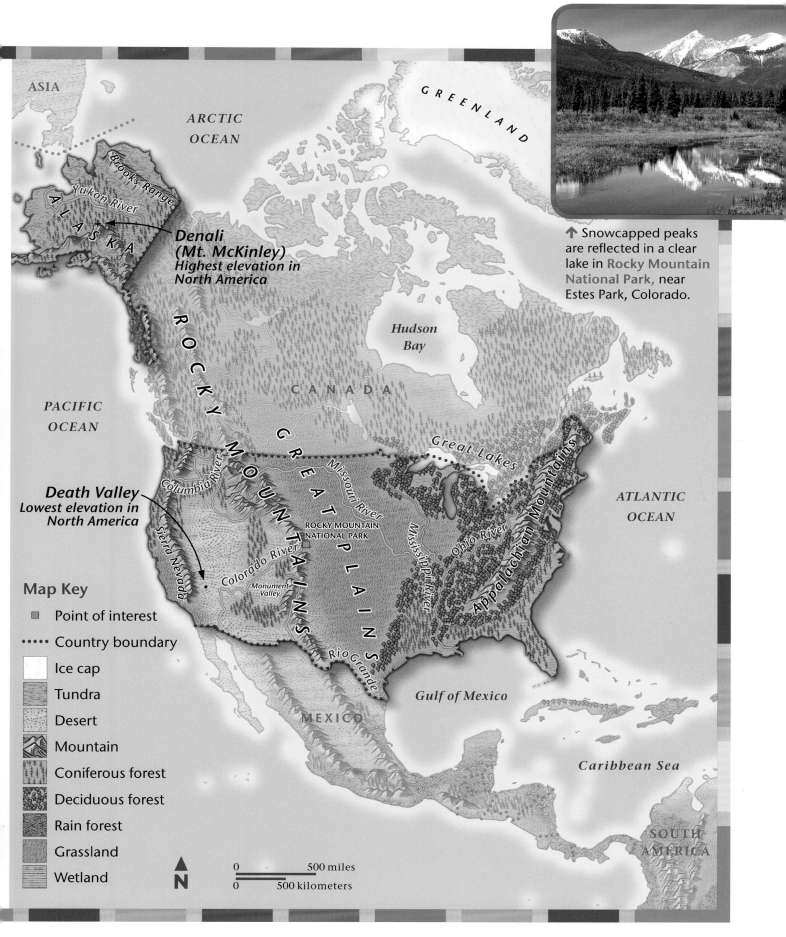

ASIA

ARCTIC OCEAN

GREENLAND

Brooks Range

ALASKA

Yukon River

Denali
(Mt. McKinley)
Highest elevation in
North America

PACIFIC OCEAN

R O C K Y   M O U N T A I N S

CANADA

Hudson Bay

Great Lakes

Columbia River

Missouri River

Death Valley
Lowest elevation in
North America

Sierra Nevada

Colorado River

Monument Valley

G R E A T   P L A I N S

ROCKY MOUNTAIN
NATIONAL PARK

Mississippi River

Ohio River

Appalachian Mountains

ATLANTIC OCEAN

Rio Grande

Gulf of Mexico

MEXICO

Caribbean Sea

SOUTH AMERICA

Snowcapped peaks
are reflected in a clear
lake in Rocky Mountain
National Park, near
Estes Park, Colorado.

Map Key

- ◼ Point of interest
- ••••• Country boundary
- Ice cap
- Tundra
- Desert
- Mountain
- Coniferous forest
- Deciduous forest
- Rain forest
- Grassland
- Wetland

N

0   500 miles
0   500 kilometers

The People

States The United States is made up of 50 states. Alaska and Hawai'i are separated from the rest of the country. So you can see them close up, they are shown in the Pacific Ocean south of California.

Cities Washington, D.C., is the national capital. Each state also has a capital city. New York City has the most people.

People The United States is made up of people from almost every country in the world. Most live and work in and around cities.

Languages English is the main language, followed by Spanish.

Products The main products include cars, machinery, petroleum, natural gas, coal, beef, wheat, and forest products.

→ Baseball is a popular sport in the United States, along with soccer, basketball, and football.

↑ Chinese New Year is a big celebration in San Francisco. Many Chinese Americans live in this California city.

Columbia River

Seattle
Olympia ★
WASHINGTON
Portland
★ Salem
OREGON
IDAHO
★ Boise
Sacramento
CALIFORNIA
★ Carson City   Salt Lake City ★
NEVADA
UT
San Francisco
San Jose
Las Vegas
ARIZO
Los Angeles
Phoenix ★
San Diego
Tucson

PACIFIC OCEAN

ALASKA
Juneau ★

| 0 | 400 miles |
| 0 | 400 kilometers |

HAWAI'I
Honolulu ★

| 0 | 150 miles |
| 0 | 150 kilometers |

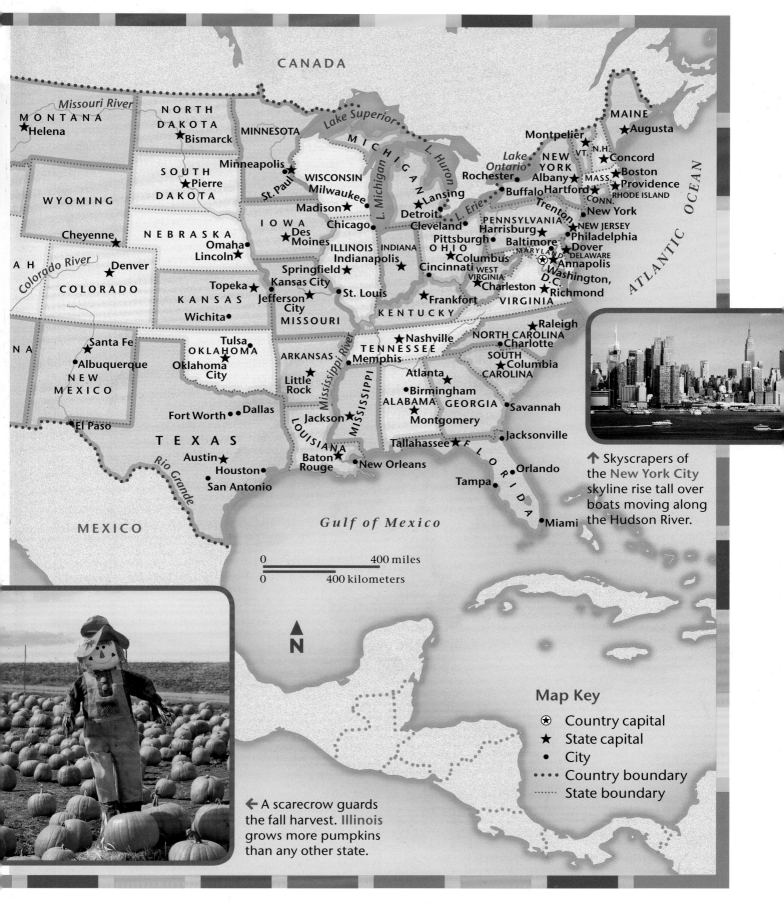

CANADA

Missouri River

MONTANA
★Helena

NORTH DAKOTA
★Bismarck

MINNESOTA

Lake Superior

MICHIGAN

L. Huron

MAINE
★Augusta

Montpelier

Lake Ontario

NEW YORK

VT.
N.H.
★Concord

WYOMING

SOUTH DAKOTA
★Pierre

Minneapolis

WISCONSIN

Rochester

Albany

MASS.
★Boston

★Providence

RHODE ISLAND

★Cheyenne

NEBRASKA

St. Paul

Milwaukee

Madison★

L. Michigan

Lansing★

Buffalo

Hartford★

CONN.

Colorado River

Omaha

Lincoln★

Des Moines

Chicago

Detroit

L. Erie

Cleveland

Trenton

New York

PENNSYLVANIA

NEW JERSEY

Philadelphia

A H

Denver★

COLORADO

IOWA

ILLINOIS

Springfield★

INDIANA

Indianapolis

OHIO

Pittsburgh

Columbus

Harrisburg★

Baltimore

Dover

DELAWARE

MARYLAND

Annapolis

NA

Santa Fe★

Topeka★

Kansas City

St. Louis

Cincinnati

WEST VIRGINIA

Washington, D.C.

Albuquerque

KANSAS

Jefferson City

Frankfort★

Charleston

Richmond

NEW MEXICO

Wichita

MISSOURI

KENTUCKY

VIRGINIA

Raleigh★

El Paso

Tulsa

OKLAHOMA

ARKANSAS

Nashville★

TENNESSEE

NORTH CAROLINA

Charlotte

Oklahoma City

Mississippi River

Memphis

SOUTH CAROLINA

Columbia

Fort Worth

Dallas

Little Rock★

Atlanta★

Birmingham

ALABAMA

GEORGIA

Savannah

TEXAS

Jackson★

MISSISSIPPI

Montgomery★

Rio Grande

Austin★

LOUISIANA

Tallahassee★

Jacksonville

Houston

Baton Rouge★

New Orleans

FLORIDA

Orlando

San Antonio

Tampa

MEXICO

Gulf of Mexico

Miami

0   400 miles
0   400 kilometers

N

ATLANTIC OCEAN

Skyscrapers of the New York City skyline rise tall over boats moving along the Hudson River.

Map Key
⊛ Country capital
★ State capital
• City
•••• Country boundary
······ State boundary

← A scarecrow guards the fall harvest. Illinois grows more pumpkins than any other state.

The National Capital: Washington, D.C.

Land & Water The National Mall, the Potomac River, and the Anacostia River are important land and water features of the District of Columbia.

Statehood The District of Columbia was founded in 1790, but it is not a state.

People & Places The District of Columbia's population is 672,228. Known as Washington, D.C., the city is the seat of the U.S. government.

Fun Fact The flag of the District of Columbia, with three red stars and two red stripes, is based on the shield in George Washington's family coat of arms.

→ The **Smithsonian Institution**, the world's largest museum, is actually made up of 19 museums and the National Zoo. Established in 1846, it is sometimes called the nation's attic because of its large collections.

← **Abraham Lincoln**, who was president during the Civil War and a strong opponent of slavery, is remembered in a memorial that houses this seated statue at the west end of the National Mall.

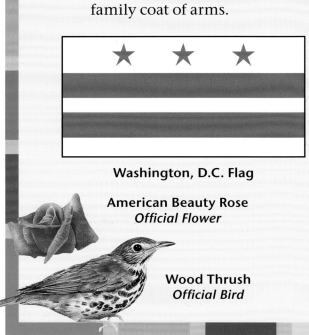

Washington, D.C. Flag

American Beauty Rose
Official Flower

Wood Thrush
Official Bird

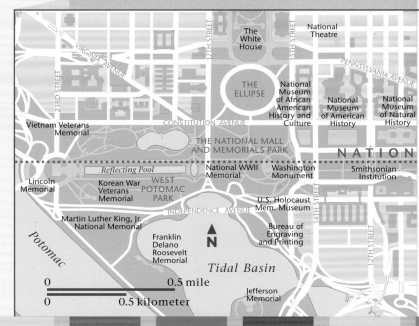

17TH STREET
The White House
National Theatre
15TH STREET
VIRGINIA AVENUE
PENNSYLVANIA AVENUE
23RD STREET
THE ELLIPSE
National Museum of African American History and Culture
National Museum of American History
National Museum of Natural History
CONSTITUTION AVENUE
Vietnam Veterans Memorial
THE NATIONAL MALL AND MEMORIALS PARK
N A T I O N
Reflecting Pool
National WWII Memorial
Washington Monument
Smithsonian Institution
Lincoln Memorial
Korean War Veterans Memorial
WEST POTOMAC PARK
14TH STREET
U.S. Holocaust Mem. Museum
INDEPENDENCE AVENUE
Martin Luther King, Jr. National Memorial
Bureau of Engraving and Printing
12TH STREET
Potomac
Franklin Delano Roosevelt Memorial
N
Tidal Basin
0 — 0.5 mile
0 — 0.5 kilometer
Jefferson Memorial

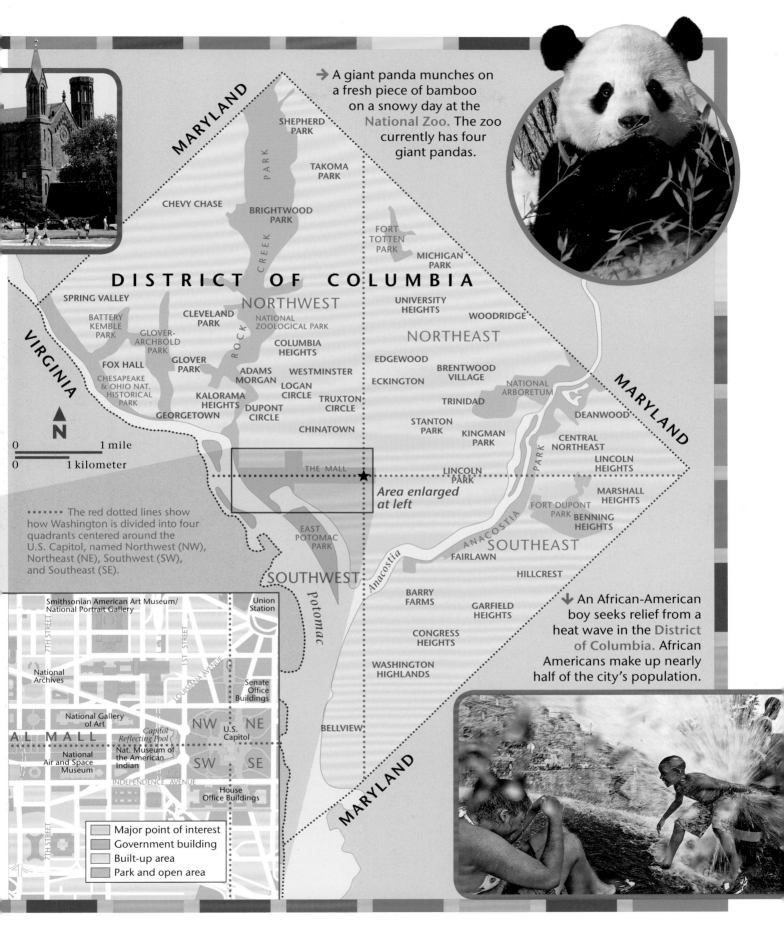

A giant panda munches on a fresh piece of bamboo on a snowy day at the National Zoo. The zoo currently has four giant pandas.

MARYLAND

VIRGINIA

DISTRICT OF COLUMBIA

NORTHWEST

NORTHEAST

SOUTHEAST

SOUTHWEST

SHEPHERD PARK

TAKOMA PARK

CHEVY CHASE

BRIGHTWOOD PARK

ROCK CREEK PARK

FORT TOTTEN PARK

MICHIGAN PARK

SPRING VALLEY

UNIVERSITY HEIGHTS

WOODRIDGE

BATTERY KEMBLE PARK

CLEVELAND PARK

NATIONAL ZOOLOGICAL PARK

GLOVER-ARCHBOLD PARK

COLUMBIA HEIGHTS

EDGEWOOD

BRENTWOOD VILLAGE

FOX HALL

GLOVER PARK

ECKINGTON

NATIONAL ARBORETUM

CHESAPEAKE & OHIO NAT. HISTORICAL PARK

ADAMS MORGAN

WESTMINSTER

TRINIDAD

KALORAMA HEIGHTS

LOGAN CIRCLE

GEORGETOWN

DUPONT CIRCLE

TRUXTON CIRCLE

STANTON PARK

KINGMAN PARK

DEANWOOD

CHINATOWN

CENTRAL NORTHEAST

LINCOLN HEIGHTS

THE MALL

LINCOLN PARK

Area enlarged at left

MARSHALL HEIGHTS

FORT DUPONT PARK

BENNING HEIGHTS

EAST POTOMAC PARK

Anacostia

ANACOSTIA PARK

SOUTHEAST

FAIRLAWN

HILLCREST

Potomac

BARRY FARMS

GARFIELD HEIGHTS

CONGRESS HEIGHTS

WASHINGTON HIGHLANDS

BELLVIEW

MARYLAND

N

0 ——— 1 mile
0 ——— 1 kilometer

•••••• The red dotted lines show how Washington is divided into four quadrants centered around the U.S. Capitol, named Northwest (NW), Northeast (NE), Southwest (SW), and Southeast (SE).

An African-American boy seeks relief from a heat wave in the District of Columbia. African Americans make up nearly half of the city's population.

Smithsonian American Art Museum/ National Portrait Gallery

Union Station

7TH STREET

1ST STREET

National Archives

LOUISIANA AVENUE

Senate Office Buildings

National Gallery of Art

Capitol Reflecting Pool

NW | NE

AL MALL

National Air and Space Museum

Nat. Museum of the American Indian

U.S. Capitol

SW | SE

INDEPENDENCE AVENUE

House Office Buildings

7TH STREET

Major point of interest
Government building
Built-up area
Park and open area

The Northeast

Early settlers and traders from Europe established colonies in the Northeast region. These colonies eventually became states. Over time, people came from countries all around the world to live in the United States. Many of these people arrived through large port cities in the Northeast, including New York City, NY, Boston, MA, and Baltimore, MD. They brought with them different customs, languages, and beliefs that make the Northeast a region of great variety. Today the Northeast region includes the country's financial center, New York City, and its political capital, Washington, D.C.

Water plunges as much as 110 feet (34 m) over the American Falls on the Niagara River near New York's northwestern border with our neighbor Canada. Black bears are common in the forests of the region.

Connecticut

Land & Water Mount Frissell, the Connecticut River, and Long Island Sound are important land and water features of Connecticut.

Statehood Connecticut became the 5th state in 1788.

People & Places Connecticut's population is 3,590,886. Hartford is the state capital. The largest city is Bridgeport.

Fun Fact The sperm whale, Connecticut's state animal, is known for its massive head. Its brain is larger than that of any other creature known to have lived on Earth.

Connecticut State Flag

Mountain Laurel
State Flower

Robin
State Bird

↑ Girls' lacrosse is popular in schools and colleges in Connecticut and across the United States. It was adapted from a Native American game.

Mt. Frissell
2,380 ft
725 m

Taconic Range

APPALACHIAN NATIONAL SCENIC TRAIL

Housatonic

MACEDONIA BROOK STATE PARK

New Milford

Lake Candlewood

NEW YORK

Danbury

Norwalk

Stamford

← The *Charles W. Morgan*, launched in 1841 and now docked in Mystic Seaport, is the only remaining wooden whaling ship in the world.

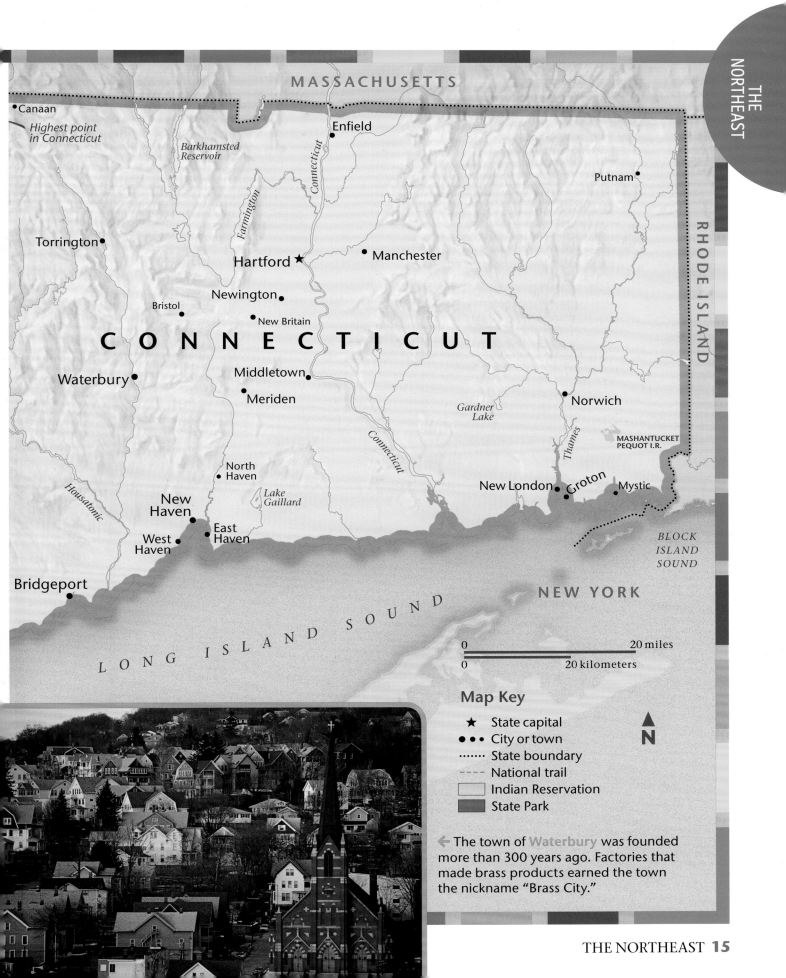

MASSACHUSETTS

•Canaan

Highest point in Connecticut

Enfield

Barkhamsted Reservoir

Connecticut

Putnam•

Torrington•

Farmington

Hartford ★

Manchester•

RHODE ISLAND

Newington•

Bristol•

CONNECTICUT

New Britain•

Waterbury•

Middletown•

Meriden•

Gardner Lake

Norwich•

Connecticut

Thames

MASHANTUCKET PEQUOT I.R.

Housatonic

North Haven•

Lake Gaillard

New Haven

West Haven•

East Haven•

New London• Groton• Mystic•

BLOCK ISLAND SOUND

Bridgeport•

NEW YORK

L O N G   I S L A N D   S O U N D

| 0 | 20 miles |
| 0 | 20 kilometers |

Map Key

★ State capital
••• City or town
······ State boundary
----- National trail
▢ Indian Reservation
▢ State Park

N

← The town of **Waterbury** was founded more than 300 years ago. Factories that made brass products earned the town the nickname "Brass City."

DELAWARE

Delaware

Land & Water The Barrier Islands, Cypress Swamp, and Delaware Bay are important land and water features of Delaware.

Statehood Delaware became the 1st state in 1787.

People & Places Delaware's population is 945,934. Dover is the state capital. The largest city is Wilmington.

Fun Fact Each year contestants bring pumpkins and launching machines to the Punkin Chunkin World Championship in Bridgeville to see who can toss their big orange squash the farthest.

↑ The Delmarva Peninsula, with more than 1,500 poultry growers, is a major producing area for chickens. The industry's trade association is located in Georgetown.

→ Patriotic boys wave American flags at a Delaware motorsports track near Delmar. Racing fans have come to the tracks since they opened in 1963.

↓ Brightly colored umbrellas dot Bethany Beach. Sun, sand, and surf attract thousands of vacationers each year to Delaware's shore.

Delaware State Flag

DECEMBER 7, 1787

Peach Blossom
State Flower

Blue Hen Chicken
State Bird

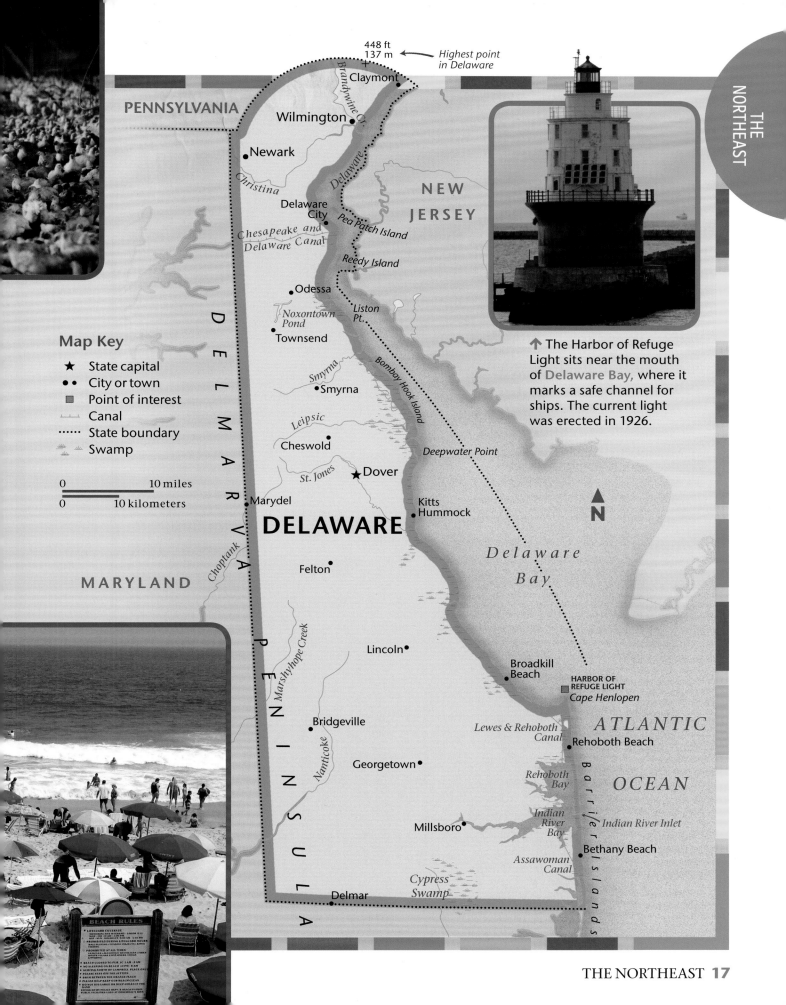

PENNSYLVANIA

448 ft
137 m ← Highest point
in Delaware

Claymont

Wilmington

Newark

Christina

Delaware

NEW
JERSEY

Delaware
City

Pea Patch Island

*Chesapeake and
Delaware Canal*

Reedy Island

Odessa

*Noxontown
Pond*

*Liston
Pt.*

Townsend

Bombay Hook Island

Smyrna

Smyrna

Leipsic

Cheswold

Deepwater Point

St. Jones

★ Dover

**The Harbor of Refuge
Light** sits near the mouth
of Delaware Bay, where it
marks a safe channel for
ships. The current light
was erected in 1926.

Map Key

★ State capital
•• City or town
■ Point of interest
Canal
•••• State boundary
Swamp

0 ——————— 10 miles
0 ——————— 10 kilometers

Marydel

DELAWARE

Kitts
Hummock

*Delaware
Bay*

N

Felton

Marshyhope Creek

Choptank

MARYLAND

Lincoln

Broadkill
Beach

HARBOR OF
REFUGE LIGHT
■ *Cape Henlopen*

*Lewes & Rehoboth
Canal*

ATLANTIC

Rehoboth Beach

Bridgeville

Nanticoke

*Rehoboth
Bay*

OCEAN

Georgetown

*Indian
River
Bay*

Indian River Inlet

Millsboro

Bethany Beach

*Assawoman
Canal*

*Cypress
Swamp*

Delmar

BEACH RULES

Maine

Land & Water
The Appalachian Mountains, Mount Katahdin, and the Gulf of Maine are important land and water features of Maine.

Statehood
Maine became the 23rd state in 1820.

People & Places
Maine's population is 1,329,328. Augusta is the state capital. The largest city is Portland.

↑ More than 60 lighthouses line Maine's rocky coastline, warning ships of danger. The oldest lighthouse, Portland Head Light, is located at Cape Elizabeth.

Fun Fact
During the last ice age, glaciers carved hundreds of bays and inlets along Maine's shoreline and created some 2,000 islands off the coast.

← Each year Rockland hosts the Maine Lobster Festival. This celebration of the state's popular seafood delicacy attracts visitors from far and near.

↓ Moose are North America's largest deer, averaging six feet (2 m) tall at the shoulders. This female stands knee-deep in grass near Rangeley Lake.

Maine State Flag

White Pine Cone and Tassel
State Flower

Chickadee
State Bird

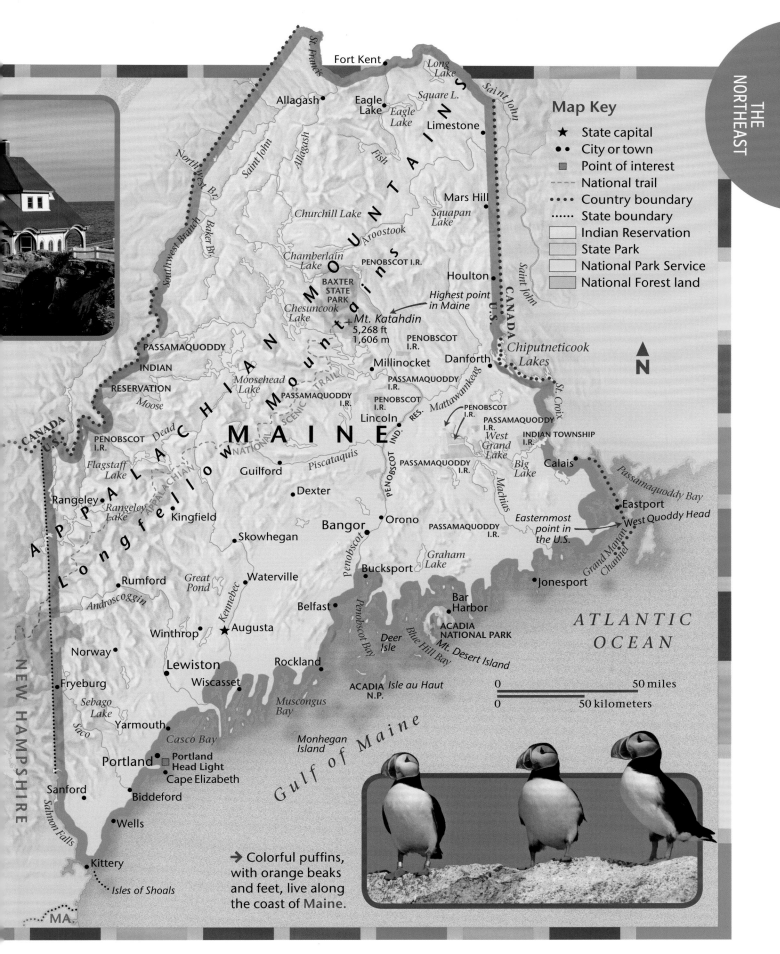

Map Key

★ State capital
•• City or town
■ Point of interest
- - - National trail
•••• Country boundary
•••• State boundary
☐ Indian Reservation
☐ State Park
☐ National Park Service
☐ National Forest land

Fort Kent

Long Lake

Allagash

Eagle Lake

Square L.

Eagle Lake

Limestone

Saint John

Saint John

Northwest Br.

Saint John

Allagash

Fish

Mars Hill

Squapan Lake

Churchill Lake

Aroostook

Baker Br.

Southwest Branch

Chamberlain Lake

PENOBSCOT I.R.

Houlton

Saint John

CANADA
U.S.

BAXTER STATE PARK

Chesuncook Lake

Highest point in Maine

+ Mt. Katahdin
5,268 ft
1,606 m

PENOBSCOT I.R.

Danforth

Chiputneticook Lakes

N

PASSAMAQUODDY

INDIAN

RESERVATION

Moosehead Lake

PASSAMAQUODDY I.R.

PENOBSCOT I.R.

PASSAMAQUODDY I.R.

Mattawamkeag

St. Croix

PENOBSCOT I.R.

PASSAMAQUODDY INDIAN TOWNSHIP

Moose

CANADA
U.S.

Dead

PENOBSCOT I.R.

Lincoln

PENOBSCOT IND. RES.

West Grand Lake

Calais

Passamaquoddy Bay

Flagstaff Lake

MAINE

Piscataquis

PASSAMAQUODDY I.R.

Big Lake

APPALACHIAN

NATIONAL

SCENIC

TRAIL

Guilford

PENOBSCOT

PASSAMAQUODDY I.R.

Eastport

Rangeley

Rangeley Lake

Dexter

Eastermost point in the U.S.

West Quoddy Head

Longfellow

Kingfield

Machias

PASSAMAQUODDY I.R.

Bangor

Orono

Grand Manan Channel

APPALACHIAN

Skowhegan

Penobscot

Graham Lake

Jonesport

A P P A L A C H I A N

Rumford

Great Pond

Waterville

Bucksport

Androscoggin

Belfast

Penobscot Bay

Bar Harbor

ATLANTIC OCEAN

Kennebec

Winthrop

★ Augusta

Rockland

Deer Isle

Blue Hill Bay

ACADIA NATIONAL PARK

Mt. Desert Island

Norway

Lewiston

Wiscasset

ACADIA N.P.

Isle au Haut

0   50 miles
0   50 kilometers

Fryeburg

Sebago Lake

Muscongus Bay

Saco

Yarmouth

Casco Bay

Monhegan Island

Gulf of Maine

NEW HAMPSHIRE

Portland
■ Portland Head Light

Cape Elizabeth

Sanford

Biddeford

Salmon Falls

Wells

Kittery

Isles of Shoals

MA.

→ Colorful puffins, with orange beaks and feet, live along the coast of Maine.

MARYLAND

Maryland

 Land & Water The Appalachian Mountains, Potomac River, and Chesapeake Bay are important land and water features of Maryland.

 Statehood Maryland became the 7th state in 1788.

People & Places Maryland's population is 6,006,401. Annapolis is the state capital. The largest city is Baltimore.

Fun Fact The name of Baltimore's professional football team—the Ravens—may have been inspired by a poem written by the famous American author Edgar Allan Poe, who lived in Baltimore in the mid-1800s.

Youghiogheny
Deep Creek Lake
Highest point in Maryland
+ Backbone Mt. 3,360 feet 1,024 meters
Cumberland
Allegheny Mountains
N. Branch
Chesapeake and
S. Branch
Ohio Canal
Potomac
APPALACHIAN
WEST VIRGINIA

↑ Sailing is a popular pastime on Maryland's Chesapeake Bay. In the background, the **Bay Bridge** stretches 4.3 miles (6.9 km) across the waters of the bay.

Maryland State Flag

Black-Eyed Susan
State Flower

Northern (Baltimore) Oriole
State Bird

↑ Since the early 1700s, Baltimore, near the upper Chesapeake Bay, has been a major seaport and a focus of trade, industry, and immigration.

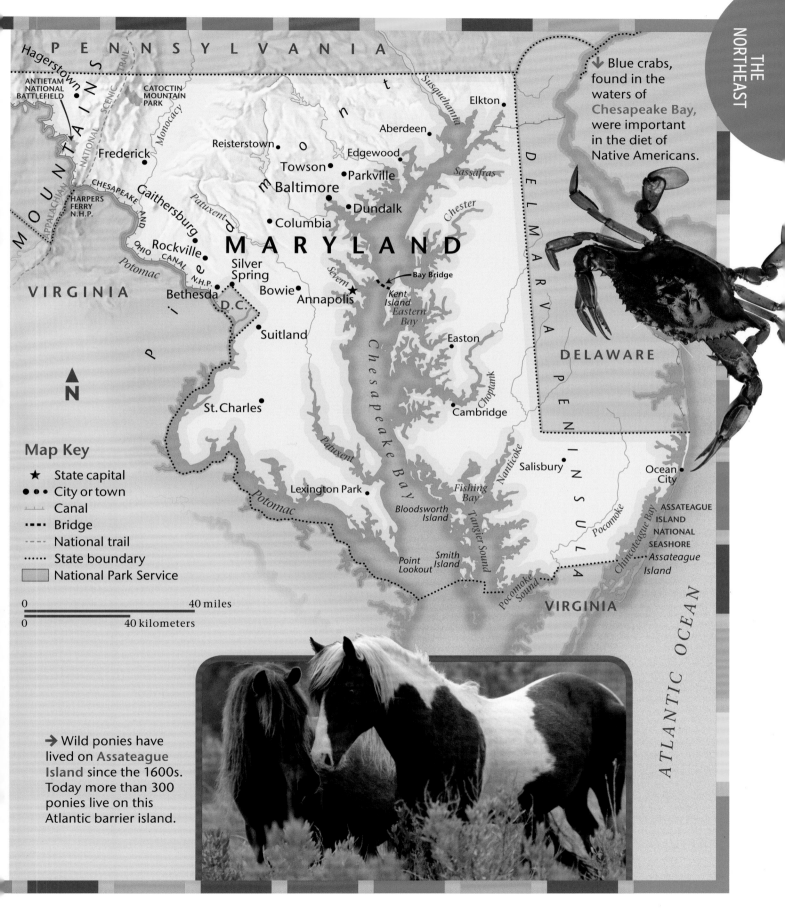

PENNSYLVANIA

Hagerstown

ANTIETAM
NATIONAL
BATTLEFIELD

CATOCTIN
MOUNTAIN
PARK

Frederick

Reisterstown

Elkton

Aberdeen

Edgewood

Towson

Parkville

Baltimore

Dundalk

Columbia

Gaithersburg

Rockville

MARYLAND

Silver
Spring

Bowie

Annapolis

Bay Bridge

Kent
Island
Eastern
Bay

Easton

VIRGINIA

Bethesda

D.C.

Suitland

St. Charles

N

Severn

Chesapeake Bay

Choptank

Cambridge

DELAWARE

Sassafras

Chester

HARPERS
FERRY
N.H.P.

CHESAPEAKE
AND
OHIO
CANAL
N.H.P.

Monocacy

Patuxent

Potomac

APPALACHIAN

NATIONAL SCENIC TRAIL

Susquehanna

↓ Blue crabs,
found in the
waters of
Chesapeake Bay,
were important
in the diet of
Native Americans.

Map Key

★ State capital
●●● City or town
Canal
Bridge
National trail
State boundary
National Park Service

Patuxent

Lexington Park

Bloodsworth
Island

Point
Lookout

Smith
Island

Fishing
Bay

Nanticoke

Tangier Sound

Salisbury

Ocean
City

ASSATEAGUE
ISLAND
NATIONAL
SEASHORE

Assateague
Island

Pocomoke

Chincoteague Bay

Pocomoke
Sound

VIRGINIA

ATLANTIC OCEAN

Potomac

0   40 miles
0   40 kilometers

→ Wild ponies have
lived on **Assateague
Island** since the 1600s.
Today more than 300
ponies live on this
Atlantic barrier island.

Massachusetts

![icon] **Land & Water** The Berkshires, Cape Cod, and Nantucket Sound are important land and water features of Massachusetts.

![icon] **Statehood** Massachusetts became the 6th state in 1788.

![icon] **People & Places** Massachusetts's population is 6,794,422. Boston is the state capital and the largest city.

![icon] **Fun Fact** In 1891 James Naismith invented the game of basketball as a form of physical activity. Today the Basketball Hall of Fame is located in Springfield in his honor.

Massachusetts State Flag

Chickadee
State Bird

Mayflower
State Flower

VERMONT

North Adams

Mt. Greylock ← Highest point in Massachusetts
3,491 ft
1,064 m

Deerfield

Greenfield

Hoosic

NEW YORK

Pittsfield

PIONEER

M A S S

Northampton

Amherst

Middle Branch

West Branch

Westfield

V A L L E Y

Holyoke

Otis Res.

Chicopee

Springfield

Housatonic

W. Branch Farmington

The Berkshires

Taconic Range

SCENIC

NATIONAL

APPALACHIAN

TRAIL

Connecticut

CONNECTICUT

↑ Fenway Park in **Boston** is home to the Red Sox major league baseball team. The park was named for a Boston neighborhood known as the Fens.

↓ Cranberries are a major agricultural crop in Massachusetts, which produces 25 percent of the cranberries grown in the United States. An annual cranberry harvest festival is held in **Wareham**.

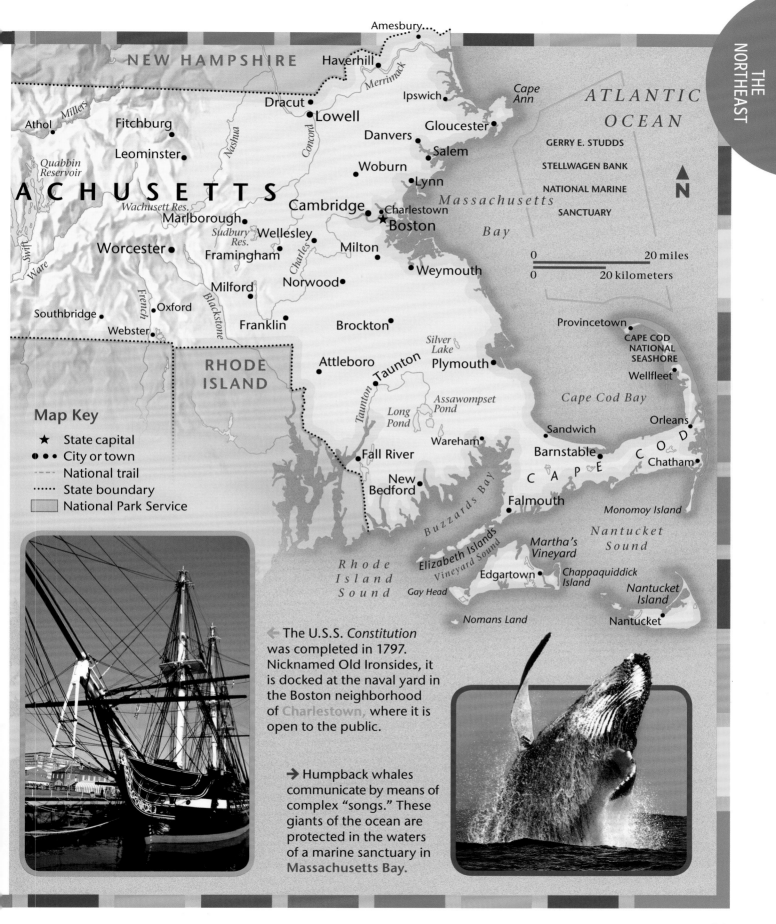

NEW HAMPSHIRE

Amesbury

Haverhill

Merrimack

Ipswich

Cape Ann

ATLANTIC OCEAN

Dracut
Lowell

Danvers

Gloucester

Athol

Fitchburg

Millers

Salem

Leominster

Nashua

Woburn

Concord

GERRY E. STUDDS

STELLWAGEN BANK

Quabbin Reservoir

Lynn

NATIONAL MARINE

ACHUSETTS

Wachusett Res.

Cambridge

Charlestown

Massachusetts

SANCTUARY

N

Marlborough

★ Boston

Bay

Wellesley

Sudbury Res.

Swift

Worcester

Milton

0   20 miles

Framingham

Charles

Weymouth

0   20 kilometers

Ware

Milford

Norwood

Southbridge

French

Oxford

Blackstone

Provincetown

Webster

Franklin

Brockton

Silver Lake

CAPE COD NATIONAL SEASHORE

RHODE ISLAND

Attleboro

Taunton

Taunton

Plymouth

Cape Cod Bay

Wellfleet

Assawompset Pond

Orleans

Map Key

★   State capital

●●●   City or town

– – –   National trail

········   State boundary

▢   National Park Service

Long Pond

Sandwich

Barnstable

C   A   P   E

C   O   D

Chatham

Wareham

Fall River

New Bedford

Buzzards Bay

Falmouth

Monomoy Island

Nantucket Sound

Rhode Island Sound

Elizabeth Islands

Vineyard Sound

Martha's Vineyard

Edgartown

Chappaquiddick Island

Nantucket Island

Gay Head

Nantucket

Nomans Land

← The U.S.S. *Constitution* was completed in 1797. Nicknamed Old Ironsides, it is docked at the naval yard in the Boston neighborhood of Charlestown, where it is open to the public.

→ Humpback whales communicate by means of complex "songs." These giants of the ocean are protected in the waters of a marine sanctuary in Massachusetts Bay.

New Hampshire

Land & Water The White Mountains, Mount Washington, and the Merrimack River are important land and water features of New Hampshire.

Statehood New Hampshire became the 9th state in 1788.

People & Places New Hampshire's population is 1,330,608. Concord is the state capital. The largest city is Manchester.

Fun Fact The first potato grown in the United States was planted in 1719 in Londonderry on the Common Field, now known simply as the Commons.

↑ A golden dome topped by a war eagle rises above New Hampshire's State House in Concord. The pale granite building was completed in 1819.

← Bitter cold and heavy snow are common in the White Mountains of New Hampshire, where snow tubing and skiing are popular winter sports.

↓ Mount Washington rises above trees rich with autumn colors. But soon winter will arrive, bringing some of the most extreme weather in the world.

New Hampshire State Flag

Purple Lilac
State Flower

Purple Finch
State Bird

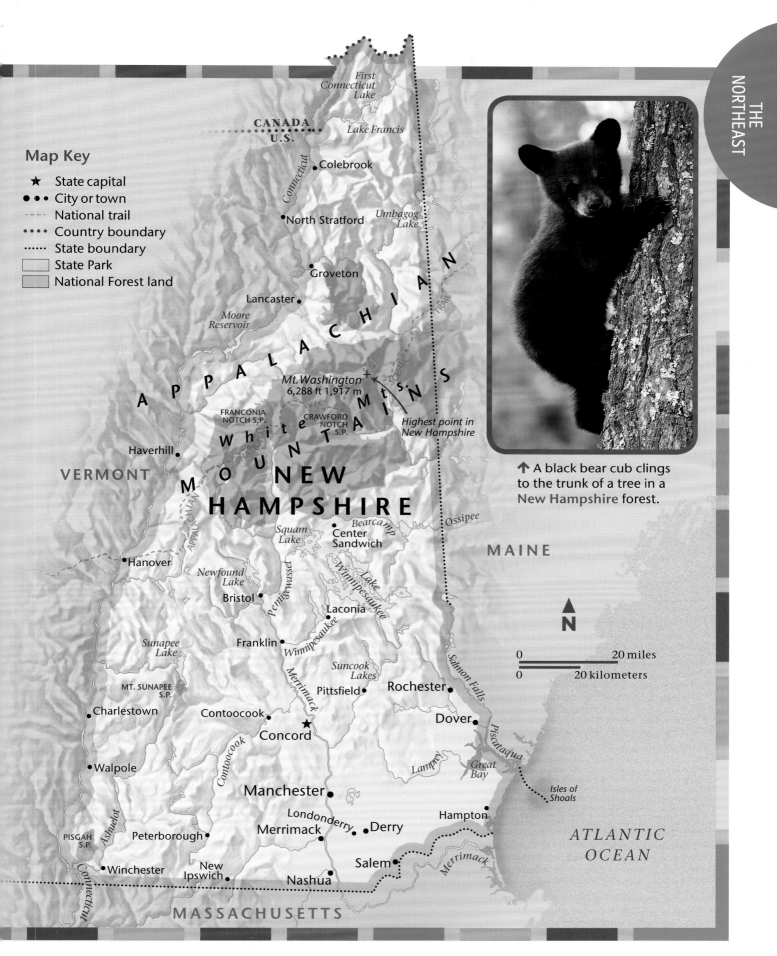

Map Key

★ State capital
●●● City or town
--- National trail
•••• Country boundary
••••• State boundary
☐ State Park
☐ National Forest land

First Connecticut Lake

Lake Francis

CANADA
U.S.

Colebrook

Connecticut

Umbagog Lake

North Stratford

Groveton

Lancaster

Moore Reservoir

APPALACHIAN

TRAIL

Mt. Washington
6,288 ft 1,917 m

FRANCONIA NOTCH S.P.

CRAWFORD NOTCH S.P.

White Mts.

MOUNTAINS

Highest point in New Hampshire

Haverhill

VERMONT

APPALACHIAN

NEW HAMPSHIRE

Squam Lake

Bearcamp

Center Sandwich

Ossipee

MAINE

Hanover

Newfound Lake

Pemigewasset

Lake Winnipesaukee

Bristol

Laconia

Sunapee Lake

Franklin

Winnipesaukee

Suncook Lakes

MT. SUNAPEE S.P.

Merrimack

Pittsfield

Rochester

Salmon Falls

Charlestown

Contoocook

Dover

Piscataqua

★ Concord

Contoocook

Lamprey

Great Bay

Walpole

Manchester

Londonderry

Hampton

ATLANTIC OCEAN

PISGAH S.P.

Ashuelot

Peterborough

Merrimack

Derry

Isles of Shoals

Winchester

New Ipswich

Salem

Merrimack

Connecticut

Nashua

MASSACHUSETTS

↑ A black bear cub clings to the trunk of a tree in a **New Hampshire** forest.

N

0 _____ 20 miles
0 _____ 20 kilometers

New Jersey

Land & Water The Kittatinny Mountains, Cape May, and the Delaware River are important land and water features of New Jersey.

Statehood New Jersey became the 3rd state in 1787.

People & Places New Jersey's population is 8,958,013. Trenton is the state capital. The largest city is Newark.

Fun Fact The first dinosaur skeleton found in North America was excavated at Haddonfield in 1858. It was named *Hadrosaurus* in honor of its discovery site.

↑ Sandy beaches on the Atlantic coast of New Jersey attract vacationers from near and far. Roller coasters are just one of the exciting rides in amusement parks along the shore.

← Street names, such as Boardwalk and Park Place, in the popular board game Monopoly are taken from actual street names in Atlantic City.

↓ The skylines of Jersey City (foreground) and New York City (in the distance at right) glow in the evening light. Jersey City, the second largest city in the state, is home to many large corporations.

New Jersey State Flag

American Goldfinch
State Bird

Violet
State Flower

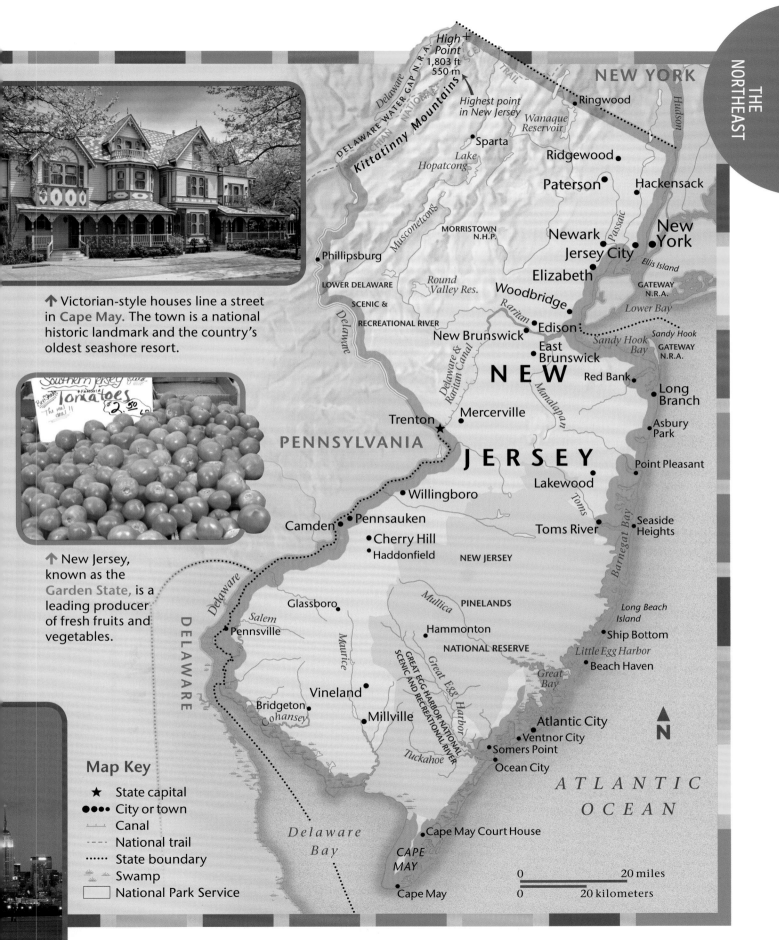

↑ Victorian-style houses line a street in **Cape May.** The town is a national historic landmark and the country's oldest seashore resort.

↑ New Jersey, known as the **Garden State,** is a leading producer of fresh fruits and vegetables.

NEW YORK

High + Point
1,803 ft
550 m

Highest point in New Jersey

Ringwood

Delaware Water Gap N.R.A.

Kittatinny Mountains

Sparta

Wanaque Reservoir

Lake Hopatcong

Ridgewood

Paterson

Hackensack

Hudson

Musconetcong

MORRISTOWN N.H.P.

Newark

New York

Jersey City

Ellis Island

Phillipsburg

LOWER DELAWARE

Round Valley Res.

Elizabeth

GATEWAY N.R.A.

Woodbridge

Lower Bay

SCENIC &

RECREATIONAL RIVER

Delaware

Raritan

Edison

Sandy Hook Bay

Sandy Hook

New Brunswick

East Brunswick

GATEWAY N.R.A.

N E W

Delaware & Raritan Canal

Red Bank

Long Branch

PENNSYLVANIA

Trenton

Mercerville

Manalapan

Asbury Park

J E R S E Y

Point Pleasant

Lakewood

Willingboro

Toms

Camden

Pennsauken

Toms River

Seaside Heights

Cherry Hill

Haddonfield

NEW JERSEY

Barnegat Bay

DELAWARE

Delaware

Glassboro

Mullica

PINELANDS

Long Beach Island

Salem

Pennsville

Hammonton

Ship Bottom

Maurice

NATIONAL RESERVE

Little Egg Harbor

GREAT EGG HARBOR NATIONAL SCENIC AND RECREATIONAL RIVER

Beach Haven

Bridgeton

Cohansey

Vineland

Great Egg Harbor

Great Bay

Millville

Atlantic City

N

Tuckahoe

Ventnor City

Somers Point

Ocean City

A T L A N T I C

O C E A N

Map Key

★ State capital

●●● City or town

⊢⊣ Canal

--- National trail

⋯ State boundary

Swamp

National Park Service

Delaware Bay

Cape May Court House

CAPE MAY

Cape May

0   20 miles

0   20 kilometers

New York

Land & Water The Adirondack Mountains, the Finger Lakes, and the Hudson River are important land and water features of New York.

Statehood New York became the 11th state in 1788.

People & Places New York's population is 19,795,791. Albany is the state capital. The largest city is New York City.

Fun Fact The Erie Canal, built in the 1820s, connected Buffalo to the Hudson River at Albany, allowing ships to travel from the Atlantic Ocean to the Great Lakes. The canal contributed to the growth of New York City as a major trade center.

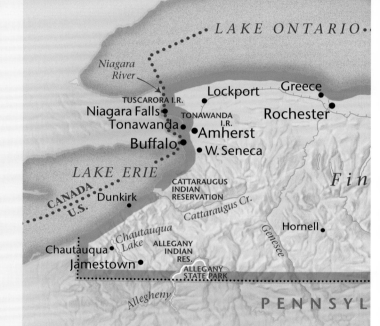

LAKE ONTARIO

Niagara River

TUSCARORA I.R.

Niagara Falls

Lockport

Greece

TONAWANDA I.R.

Tonawanda

Rochester

Amherst

Buffalo

W. Seneca

LAKE ERIE

CATTARAUGUS INDIAN RESERVATION

CANADA
U.S.

Dunkirk

Cattaraugus Cr.

Fin

Hornell

Chautauqua Lake

ALLEGANY INDIAN RES.

Genesee

Chautauqua

Jamestown

ALLEGANY STATE PARK

Allegheny

PENNSYL

New York State Flag

Eastern Bluebird
State Bird

Rose
State Flower

DISCOVERY 150

← Fresh, juicy apples are on display at a roadside stand near Chautauqua. New York is the second largest producer of apples in the United States.

CANADA
U.S.
ST. REGIS I.R.

Malone

Plattsburgh

Lake Champlain

St. Lawrence

Ogdensburg

Thousand Islands

Lake Placid

A d i r o n d a c k

→ Mt. Marcy
5,344 ft
1,629 m

Raquette

Highest point in New York

ADIRONDACK

CANADA
U.S.

Watertown

M o u n t a i n s

Lake George

PARK

Hudson

VERMONT

Black

Oswego

Glens Falls

Oneida Lake

Rome

Great Sacandaga Lake

Oswego

Utica

Saratoga Springs

Erie Canal

Syracuse

Mohawk

Erie Canal

Schenectady

ONONDAGA INDIAN RESERVATION

Auburn

Seneca Lake

ger Lakes

Cayuga Lake

Cooperstown

Troy

Albany ★

Taconic Ranges

MASSACHUSETTS

N E W Y O R K

Keuka Lake

Ithaca

Watkins Glen

Susquehanna

W. Br. Delaware

Catskill

Hudson

Catskill

Chemung

Elmira

Binghamton

Catskill Mountains

A P P A L A C H I A N

E. Branch

CATSKILL PARK

+ Slide Mt.
4,180 ft
1,274 m

Hudson

Taconic Scenic

CONNECTICUT

VANIA

Susquehanna

UPPER DELAWARE SCENIC AND RECREATIONAL RIVER

Newburgh

Poughkeepsie

← Once seriously polluted, the Gowanus Canal, in the Brooklyn area of New York City, has been undergoing cleaning efforts. Here, people canoe and enjoy the view from the water.

Middletown

Delaware

↑ Standing in New York Harbor, the Statue of Liberty, a gift from the people of France, is a symbol of freedom and democracy.

RHODE ISLAND

Block Island Sound

Long Island Sound

Montauk Point

Spring Valley

NATIONAL SCENIC

APPALACHIAN

Yonkers

New Rochelle

Huntington

Southampton

New York

Brentwood

FIRE ISLAND NATIONAL SEASHORE

Freeport

New York Harbor →

Gowanus Canal

NEW JERSEY

Staten Island

GATEWAY N.R.A.

Long Beach

Long Island

ATLANTIC OCEAN

Map Key

N

★ State capital
••• City or town
▪ Point of interest
⊔ Canal
- - - National trail
•••• Country boundary

······ State boundary
☐ Indian Reservation
☐ State Park
☐ National Park Service
☐ National Forest land

0 _____ 50 miles
0 _____ 50 kilometers

Pennsylvania

Land & Water The Allegheny Mountains, the Pocono Mountains, and the Susquehanna River are important land and water features of Pennsylvania.

Statehood Pennsylvania became the 2nd state in 1787.

People & Places Pennsylvania's population is 12,802,503. Harrisburg is the state capital. The largest city is Philadelphia.

Fun Fact The town of Hershey is known as the Chocolate Capital of the World. The Hershey Company exports its chocolate candies to some 70 countries around the world.

Pennsylvania State Flag

Mountain Laurel
State Flower

Ruffed Grouse
State Bird

LAKE ERIE ● Erie

Corry ●

Allegheny Reservoir

Meadville ●
Titusville ●

Pymatuning Reservoir

Allegheny

● Greenville

Clarion

OHIO

● Sharon

Clarion ●

Beaver

Punxsutawney

● New Castle

P E N

Ohio

● Kittanning

Allegheny

● Indiana

● McCandless

Conemaugh

Pittsburgh ●
● Penn Hills

Johnstown ●

● Washington

Highest point in Pennsylvania

A l l e g h

● Morrisville

Monongahela

● Uniontown

Mt. Davis
3,213 ft
979 m

Youghiogheny

Cheat

WEST VIRGINIA

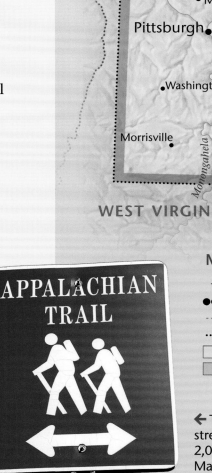

APPALACHIAN TRAIL

Map Key

★ State capital
●●●● City or town
– – – National trail
⋯⋯ State boundary
☐ National Park Service
☐ National Forest land

← The **Appalachian Trail** stretches across more than 2,000 miles (3,200 km) from Maine to Georgia. The trail passes through 14 states, including Pennsylvania.

NEW YORK

Chemung

Susquehanna

Bradford

Allegheny

Coudersport

Mansfield

Wellsboro

Sayre

Towanda

Tioga

Pine Creek

Pine Creek Gorge

St.Marys

M O U N T A I N S

UPPER DELAWARE SCENIC AND RECREATIONAL RIVER

Delaware

Carbondale

Scranton

Lake Wallenpaupack

Williamsport

West Branch Susquehanna

Wilkes-Barre

Pocono Mts.

DELAWARE WATER GAP NATIONAL RECREATION AREA

Lock Haven

Clearfield

Bloomsburg

Susquehanna

P E N N S Y L V A N I A

Mountains

Stroudsburg

Sunbury

Lehigh

State College

Pottsville

B l u e

Bethlehem

Easton

NEW JERSEY

Altoona

Mountain

Allentown

M o u n t a i n s

Juniata

SCENIC

NATIONAL

TRAIL

Reading

Doylestown

A P P A L A C H I A N

Raystown Lake

Tuscarora Mountain

Schuylkill

Delaware

Hershey

★ Harrisburg

Norristown

Levittown

Carlisle

Three Mile Island

Elizabethtown

VALLEY FORGE N.H.P.

APPALACHIAN

Bedford

Lancaster

Upper Darby

Philadelphia

Chambersburg

York

Susquehanna

Chester

Waynesboro

Gettysburg

GETTYSBURG N.H.P.

DELAWARE

A P

MARYLAND

W. VA.

0 ——— 40 miles

0 ——— 40 kilometers

N ↑

← **Pittsburgh** was established in 1758 where the Monongahela and Allegheny Rivers meet to form the Ohio River. Today it is a center of finance, medicine, education, and robotics.

→ The Liberty Bell, cast in 1753 by Pennsylvania craftsmen, hangs in Philadelphia. Because of a crack, it is no longer rung.

Rhode Island

Land & Water Block Island and Narragansett Bay, with its many islands, are important land and water features of Rhode Island.

Statehood Rhode Island became the 13th state in 1790.

People & Places Rhode Island's population is 1,056,298. Providence is the state capital and the largest city.

Fun Fact Rhode Island is the smallest U.S. state in size. It measures just 48 miles (77 km) from north to south and 37 miles (60 km) from east to west.

↑ Sailing is a popular sport in Rhode Island. This boat is in full sail on a late summer day on Narragansett Bay.

← The North Lighthouse on the northern tip of Block Island still warns ships of dangerous waters. The building, constructed in 1867, does not have a typical lighthouse design.

Rhode Island State Flag

Violet
State Flower

Rhode Island Red
State Bird

↓ Rhode Island has cold, snowy winters. Skaters enjoy ice-skating on City Center public rink in front of the historic city hall in Providence.

MASSACHUSETTS

Wallum Lake

Woonsocket

*Pawtucket
Reservoir*

Ashton

Harrisville

*Pascoag
Lake*

*Woonasquatucket
Reservoir*

Chepachet

Blackstone

*Ponaganset
Reservoir*

Greenville

Woonasquatucket

Pawtucket

North
Providence

Seekonk

+ Jerimoth Hill
812 ft 247 m

Providence ★

*Highest point
in Rhode Island*

East Providence

Ponaganset

Foster
Center

*Scituate
Reservoir*

Cranston

Pawtuxet

Providence

R H O D E

Warwick

Warren

Palmer

Bristol

Moosup

Rice City

West
Warwick

Mount Hope Bay

I S L A N D

*Flat River
Reservoir*

*Tiogue
Lake*

East
Greenwich

Narragansett Bay

*Stafford
Pond*

Tiverton

*Prudence
Island*

Portsmouth

*Nonquit
Pond*

Austin

*Conanicut
Island*

*Rhode
Island*

Sakonnet

Adamsville

Queen

Allenton

Jamestown

Newport

Hope
Valley

Kingston

Wood

*Great
Swamp*

*Sakonnet
Point*

Wakefield

Worden Pond

Ashaway

*Point
Judith
Pond*

Rhode Island Sound

NARRAGANSETT
INDIAN
RESERVATION

Pawcatuck

*Watchaug
Pond*

Charlestown

Ninigret Pond

Point Judith

*Quonochontaug
Pond*

Watch Hill

Napatree Point

**Block Island
Sound**

Sandy Point

*A T L A N T I C
O C E A N*

Block
Island

New Shoreham

Map Key

★ State capital
•• City or town
⋯⋯ State boundary
Swamp
Indian Reservation

0   10 miles
0   10 kilometers

N

CONNECTICUT

→ Coyotes are
an increasingly
common sight in
Rhode Island. They
move about mainly
in the early morning
or in the evening.

Vermont

Land & Water The Green Mountains, Lake Champlain, and the Connecticut River are important land and water features of Vermont.

Statehood Vermont became the 14th state in 1791.

People & Places Vermont's population is 626,042. Montpelier is the state capital. The largest city is Burlington.

Fun Fact From the end of the Revolutionary War until 1791, Vermont was an independent republic with its own government and money. It even thought about uniting with Canada.

↑ Vermont ice cream is famous worldwide. The headquarters of Ben & Jerry's in **Burlington** is the number one tourist attraction in the state.

Vermont State Flag

Red Clover
State Flower

Hermit Thrush
State Bird

↑ People collect the sap of maple trees, which is boiled to make maple sugar and syrup. Maple production is celebrated each year at a festival in **Tunbridge**.

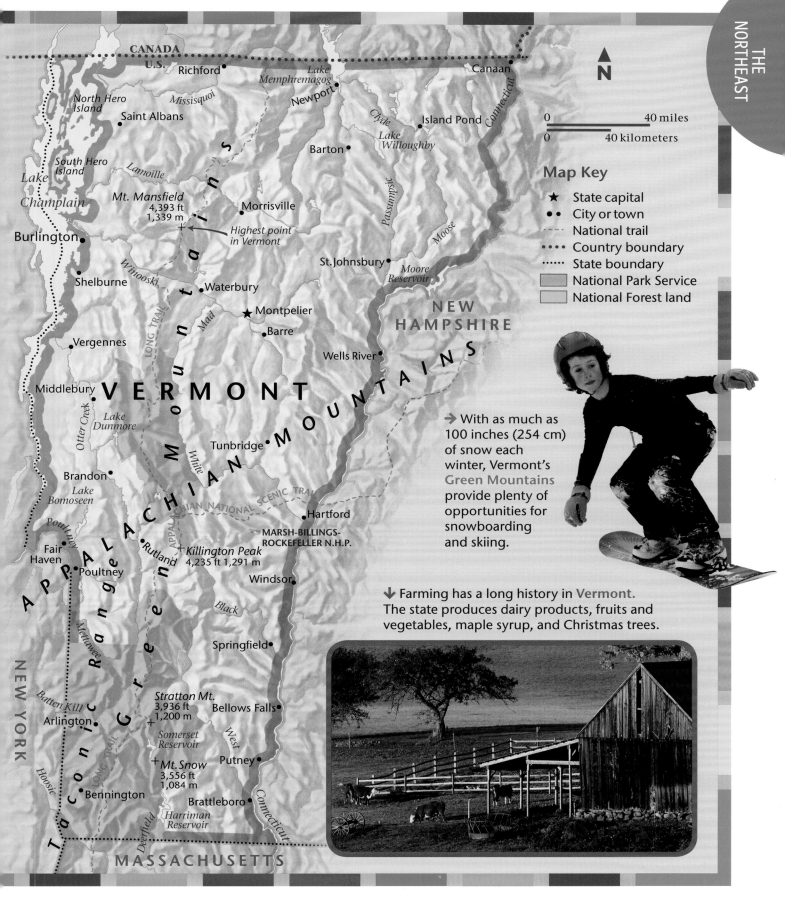

CANADA
U.S.

Richford

Lake Memphremagog

Newport

Canaan

North Hero Island

Saint Albans

Missisquoi

Island Pond

Connecticut

N

0   40 miles
0   40 kilometers

South Hero Island

Lamoille

Barton

Lake Willoughby

Clyde

Map Key

Lake Champlain

Mt. Mansfield
4,393 ft
1,339 m

Morrisville

Passumpsic

Moose

★ State capital
•• City or town
--- National trail
••• Country boundary
····· State boundary
National Park Service
National Forest land

Burlington

Highest point in Vermont

St. Johnsbury

Moore Reservoir

Shelburne

Winooski

Waterbury

Mad

Montpelier

Barre

NEW HAMPSHIRE

Vergennes

Wells River

Middlebury

V E R M O N T

Lake Dunmore

Otter Creek

White

Tunbridge •

MOUNTAINS

→ With as much as 100 inches (254 cm) of snow each winter, Vermont's **Green Mountains** provide plenty of opportunities for snowboarding and skiing.

Brandon

Lake Bomoseen

APPALACHIAN

Poultney

Hartford

MARSH-BILLINGS-ROCKEFELLER N.H.P.

SCENIC TRAIL

APPALACHIAN NATIONAL

Fair Haven

Rutland

+ **Killington Peak**
4,235 ft 1,291 m

Green

Poultney

Windsor

Black

Springfield •

Mettowee

Range

NEW YORK

Taconic

Batten Kill

Arlington

Stratton Mt.
3,936 ft
1,200 m

Bellows Falls •

Somerset Reservoir

West

↓ Farming has a long history in **Vermont**. The state produces dairy products, fruits and vegetables, maple syrup, and Christmas trees.

Hoosic

LONG TRAIL

+ Mt. Snow
3,556 ft
1,084 m

Putney •

Bennington

Brattleboro •

Connecticut

Harriman Reservoir

Deerfield

MASSACHUSETTS

The Southeast

The Southeast region of the United States is full of variety, both in its landscape and in its history. The Appalachian Mountains are old and worn down. The coastal margins are marked by barrier islands and wetlands. And in the western part of the region, the Mississippi River flows out through a broad delta into the Gulf of Mexico. The region, with roots in agriculture, suffered great destruction during the Civil War, but today it is a part of the Sunbelt, where cities are growing rapidly and the economy is shifting to high-tech industries.

Live oak trees, some hundreds of years old, form a natural arch across a country road in Georgia. These trees, draped in Spanish moss, are common in the coastal Southeast. Flamingos are a familiar sight in parks in Florida.

ALABAMA

Alabama

Land & Water The Appalachian Mountains, the Cumberland Plateau, and Mobile Bay are important land and water features of Alabama.

Statehood Alabama became the 22nd state in 1819.

People & Places Alabama's population is 4,858,979. Montgomery is the state capital. The largest city is Birmingham.

Fun Fact In Magnolia Springs, on Mobile Bay, mail is delivered by boat. This city has the country's only year-round, all-water mail route used by the U.S. Postal Service.

Alabama State Flag

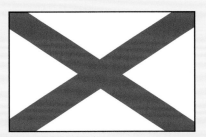

Northern Flicker
State Bird

Camellia
State Flower

↑ Southern Alabama has a narrow coastline fronting the Gulf of Mexico. The beach resort of Gulf Shores is a popular tourist destination.

↑ A welder repairs a boat in Bayou La Batre on Alabama's Gulf coast. The town is a center for shipbuilding and seafood processing.

↓ This old railroad bridge, built in 1839, was a toll bridge across the Tennessee River. Today it is a pedestrian bridge.

Map Key

★ State capital
• • • City or town
⋯⋯⋯ State boundary
National Park Service
National Forest land

The bobwhite quail is common throughout Alabama. It builds its nest on the ground and lives on a diet of seeds.

TENNESSEE

Pickwick Lake
Wilson Lake
Florence
Tennessee
Wheeler Lake
Madison
Huntsville
Decatur
Russellville

Guntersville Lake

Cumberland Plateau

APPALACHIAN MTS.

Tennessee

LITTLE RIVER CANYON NATIONAL PRESERVE

GEORGIA

Bear Creek

Cullman

Mulberry Fork
Locust Fork

Weiss Lake

Lewis Smith Lake

Gadsden

Winfield

Anniston

Cheaha Mt. 2,407 ft 734 m +
Highest point in Alabama

Tombigbee

Birmingham

Sipsey

Bessemer Hoover Talladega

Coosa

Chattahoochee

Tuscaloosa

Black Warrior

ALABAMA

Clanton

Lake Martin

West Point Lake

York

Cahaba

Selma

Auburn

Tuskegee

Phenix City

MISSISSIPPI

Black Belt

Tallapoosa

★ Montgomery

Alabama

Union Springs

Thomasville

William "Bill" Dannelly Reservoir

Greenville

Troy

Eufaula

Walter F. George Reservoir

Tombigbee

Monroeville

Conecuh

Pea

Andalusia

Choctawhatchee

Dothan

Chattahoochee

Alabama

Atmore

Conecuh

Geneva

Mobile

N

0   50 miles
0   50 kilometers

Prichard
Mobile
Bayou La Batre
Tensaw
Fairhope
Magnolia Springs
Perdido
Mobile Bay

FLORIDA

Mississippi Sound
Dauphin Island
Gulf Shores
Intracoastal Waterway

GULF OF MEXICO

Arkansas

↑ Located in the River Market District of **Little Rock,** the Museum of Discovery offers children interactive experiences in science, technology, engineering, and math.

Land & Water The Ouachita Mountains, the Ozark Plateau, and the Mississippi River are important land and water features of Arkansas.

Statehood Arkansas became the 25th state in 1836.

People & Places Arkansas has a population of 2,978,204. Little Rock is the state capital and the largest city.

Fun Fact In 1924 Crater of Diamonds State Park near Murfreesboro yielded the largest natural diamond ever found in the United States. The stone, called "Uncle Sam," weighed more than 40 carats.

Arkansas State Flag

Apple Blossom
State Flower

Mockingbird
State Bird

↑ A farmer in eastern Arkansas checks the progress of his rice crop. The state is a leading producer of rice.

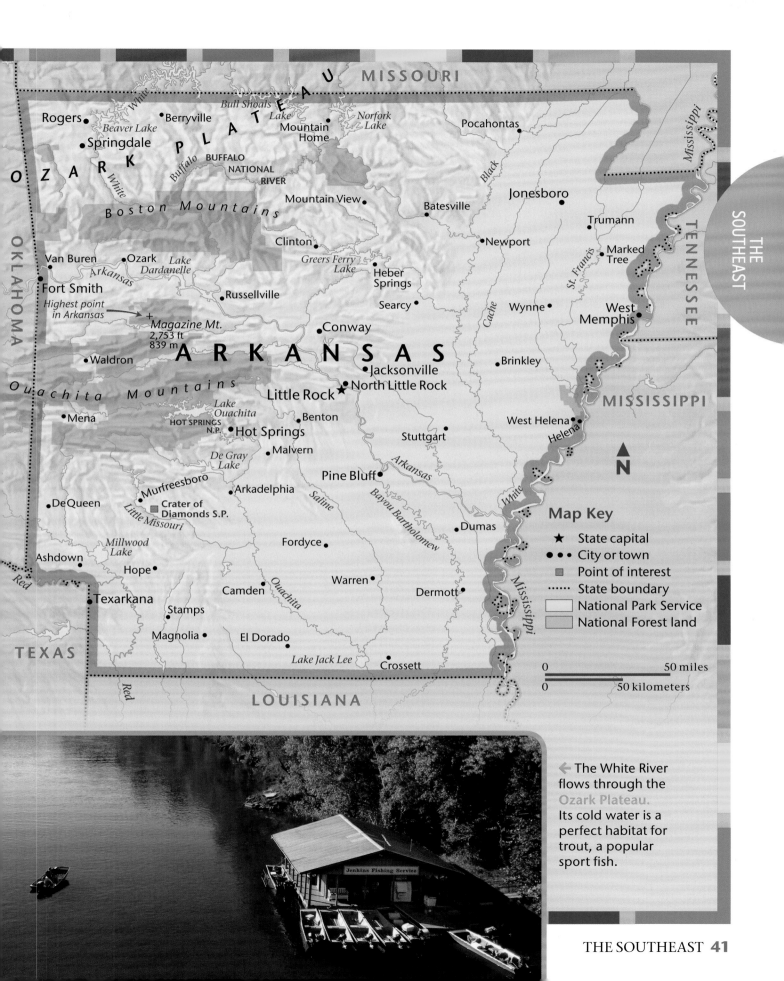

MISSOURI

OZARK PLATEAU

Rogers
Beaver Lake
Berryville
Springdale

Bull Shoals Lake
Mountain Home
Norfork Lake

Pocahontas

White

Buffalo
BUFFALO NATIONAL RIVER
White

Boston Mountains

Mountain View

Batesville

Jonesboro

Black

Trumann

Marked Tree

Clinton

Newport

St. Francis

Van Buren
Ozark
Lake Dardanelle

Greers Ferry Lake
Heber Springs

Wynne

West Memphis

Arkansas
Fort Smith
Highest point in Arkansas

Russellville

Searcy

Cache

Magazine Mt.
2,753 ft
839 m

Conway

A R K A N S A S

Brinkley

MISSISSIPPI

Waldron

Jacksonville
Little Rock
North Little Rock

Ouachita Mountains

Lake Ouachita
HOT SPRINGS N.P.
Hot Springs

Benton

Stuttgart

West Helena
Helena

N

Mena

De Gray Lake
Malvern

Arkansas

Murfreesboro
Crater of Diamonds S.P.
Little Missouri

Arkadelphia

Pine Bluff

Saline

Bayou Bartholomew

White

Map Key

DeQueen

Fordyce

★ State capital
••• City or town
■ Point of interest
····· State boundary
☐ National Park Service
☐ National Forest land

Millwood Lake

Ashdown

Hope

Warren

Dumas

Camden

Ouachita

Dermott

Mississippi

Red

Texarkana

Stamps

Magnolia

El Dorado

0   50 miles
0   50 kilometers

TEXAS

Lake Jack Lee

Crossett

Red

LOUISIANA

OKLAHOMA

TENNESSEE

Mississippi

← The White River
flows through the
Ozark Plateau.
Its cold water is a
perfect habitat for
trout, a popular
sport fish.

Jenkins Fishing Service

FLORIDA

Florida

A L A B A M A
Highest point in Florida → ✛ Britton Hill 345 ft 105 m
Pendido
Pensacola •
Fort Walton Beach
GULF ISLANDS NATIONAL SEASHORE
Panama City •

![river icon] **Land & Water** The Florida Keys, the Everglades, and Lake Okeechobee are important land and water features of Florida.

![flag icon] **Statehood** Florida became the 27th state in 1845.

![person icon] **People & Places** Florida's population is 20,271,272. Tallahassee is the state capital. The largest city is Jacksonville.

![question mark icon] **Fun Fact** Everglades National Park is home to rare and endangered species such as the American crocodile, the Florida panther, and the West Indian manatee.

⬇ The manatee is the state marine mammal of **Florida.** It averages ten feet (3 m) in length and can weigh 1,000 pounds (450 kg).

⬇ NASA's new Space Launch System, the most powerful rocket in history, will lift off from **Kennedy Space Center** in 2018.

Florida State Flag

Orange Blossom
State Flower

Mockingbird
State Bird

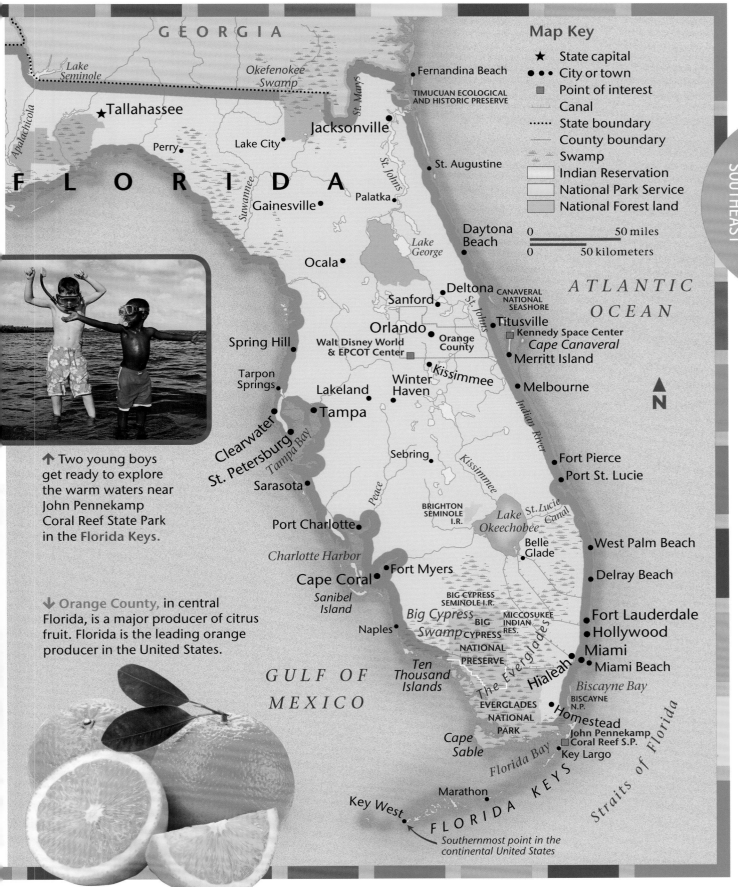

Map Key

★ State capital
••• City or town
◼ Point of interest
— Canal
···· State boundary
— County boundary
Swamp
Indian Reservation
National Park Service
National Forest land

0   50 miles
0   50 kilometers

GEORGIA

Lake Seminole

Okefenokee Swamp

★Tallahassee

Perry•

Apalachicola

F L O R I D A

Lake City•

Jacksonville

Fernandina Beach•

TIMUCUAN ECOLOGICAL AND HISTORIC PRESERVE

St. Marys

St. Augustine•

Gainesville•

Palatka•

St. Johns

Suwannee

Ocala•

Lake George

Daytona Beach•

Deltona•

Sanford•

CANAVERAL NATIONAL SEASHORE

Orlando•

Titusville•

Kennedy Space Center ◼

Cape Canaveral

Spring Hill•

Walt Disney World & EPCOT Center ◼

Orange County

Merritt Island•

St. Johns

A T L A N T I C
O C E A N

Tarpon Springs•

Kissimmee•

Melbourne•

Lakeland•

Winter Haven•

Clearwater•

•Tampa

Tampa Bay

Sebring•

Indian River

N

St. Petersburg•

Sarasota•

Peace

Kissimmee

Fort Pierce•
Port St. Lucie•

Port Charlotte•

BRIGHTON SEMINOLE I.R.

Lake Okeechobee

St. Lucie Canal

Belle Glade•

West Palm Beach•

Charlotte Harbor

•Fort Myers

Cape Coral•

Sanibel Island

BIG CYPRESS SEMINOLE I.R.

Delray Beach•

Big Cypress Swamp

BIG CYPRESS

MICCOSUKEE INDIAN RES.

Fort Lauderdale•
Hollywood•

Naples•

NATIONAL PRESERVE

The Everglades

Miami•
Miami Beach•

G U L F   O F
M E X I C O

Ten Thousand Islands

Hialeah•

Biscayne Bay

EVERGLADES NATIONAL PARK

BISCAYNE N.P.

Homestead•

Cape Sable

John Pennekamp Coral Reef S.P. ◼

Key Largo•

Florida Bay

Straits of Florida

Marathon•

F L O R I D A   K E Y S

Key West•

← Southernmost point in the continental United States

↑ Two young boys get ready to explore the warm waters near John Pennekamp Coral Reef State Park in the **Florida Keys.**

↓ **Orange County,** in central Florida, is a major producer of citrus fruit. Florida is the leading orange producer in the United States.

Georgia

← Built for the 1996 Olympic Games, Centennial Olympic Park in **Atlanta** is the site of festivals and community events that attract an estimated three million visitors each year.

Land & Water The Sea Islands, the Okefenokee Swamp, and the Savannah River are important land and water features of Georgia.

Statehood Georgia became the 4th state in 1788.

People & Places Georgia's population is 10,214,860. Atlanta is the state capital and the largest city.

Fun Fact The Georgia Aquarium in Atlanta is the largest aquarium in the world. It features more than 100,000 animals living in more than eight million gallons (30.3 million L) of water.

→ Nearly half the peanut crop in the United States is grown in Georgia. **Sylvester** is the peanut capital of the world.

↓ Alligators, which can live more than 50 years, are found in marshes, rivers, and swamps, including those in the Okefenokee National Wildlife Refuge.

Georgia State Flag

Cherokee Rose
State Flower

Brown Thrasher
State Bird

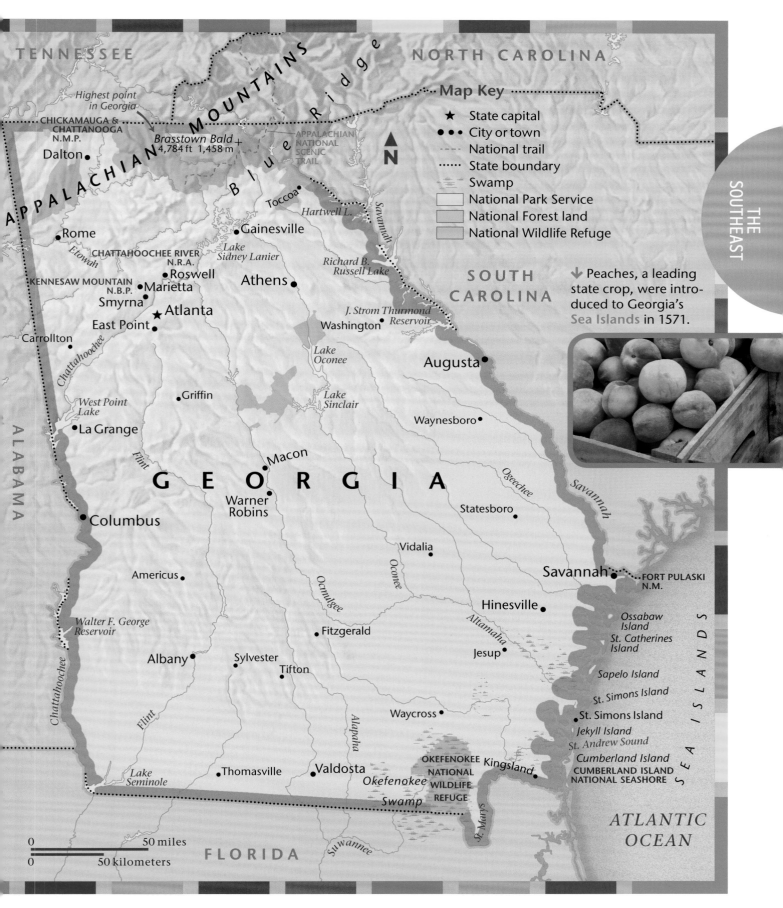

TENNESSEE

NORTH CAROLINA

*Highest point
in Georgia*

CHICKAMAUGA &
CHATTANOOGA
N.M.P.

Dalton

Brasstown Bald
4,784 ft 1,458 m

APPALACHIAN
NATIONAL
SCENIC
TRAIL

A P P A L A C H I A N   M O U N T A I N S

B l u e   R i d g e

N

Map Key

★ State capital
••• City or town
– – – National trail
······ State boundary
         Swamp
☐ National Park Service
☐ National Forest land
☐ National Wildlife Refuge

THE
SOUTHEAST

Rome

Etowah

CHATTAHOOCHEE RIVER
N.R.A.

KENNESAW MOUNTAIN
N.B.P.

Roswell

Marietta

Smyrna

★ Atlanta

East Point

Carrollton

Chattahoochee

Toccoa

Hartwell L.

Savannah

Gainesville

*Lake
Sidney Lanier*

Athens

*Richard B.
Russell Lake*

SOUTH
CAROLINA

*J. Strom Thurmond
Reservoir*

Washington

*Lake
Oconee*

Augusta

*Lake
Sinclair*

Waynesboro

↓ Peaches, a leading
state crop, were intro-
duced to Georgia's
Sea Islands in 1571.

Griffin

*West Point
Lake*

La Grange

G E O R G I A

Macon

Warner
Robins

Flint

Columbus

Ogeechee

Savannah

Statesboro

Vidalia

Oconee

Americus

Ocmulgee

Savannah

FORT PULASKI
N.M.

*Walter F. George
Reservoir*

Hinesville

Altamaha

*Ossabaw
Island*

*St. Catherines
Island*

Fitzgerald

Jesup

Sapelo Island

Albany

Sylvester

Tifton

St. Simons Island

• St. Simons Island

Jekyll Island

St. Andrew Sound

Waycross

Alapaha

S E A   I S L A N D S

Cumberland Island

CUMBERLAND ISLAND
NATIONAL SEASHORE

Chattahoochee

OKEFENOKEE
NATIONAL
WILDLIFE
REFUGE

Kingsland

Thomasville

Valdosta

*Okefenokee
Swamp*

Flint

*Lake
Seminole*

St. Marys

ATLANTIC
OCEAN

0 ————— 50 miles
0 ————— 50 kilometers

FLORIDA

Suwannee

Kentucky

![Land & Water icon] **Land & Water** Mammoth Cave, Lake Cumberland, and the Ohio River are important land and water features of Kentucky.

![Statehood icon] **Statehood** Kentucky became the 15th state in 1792.

![People & Places icon] **People & Places** Kentucky's population is 4,425,092. Frankfort is the state capital. The largest city is Louisville.

![Fun Fact icon] **Fun Fact** The song "Happy Birthday to You," one of the most popular songs in the English language, was written in 1893 by two sisters living in Louisville.

Kentucky State Flag

Goldenrod
State Flower

Cardinal
State Bird

→ Shaker Village in **Pleasant Hill** preserves the culture and history of this important social movement.

← Abraham Lincoln, the 16th U.S. president, was born near **Hodgenville.** His profile appears on the penny.

IN GOD WE TRUST · LIBERTY · 2006 D

↓ The setting sun turns the sky red over **Cave Run Lake.** The lake is a popular vacation spot because of its natural beauty.

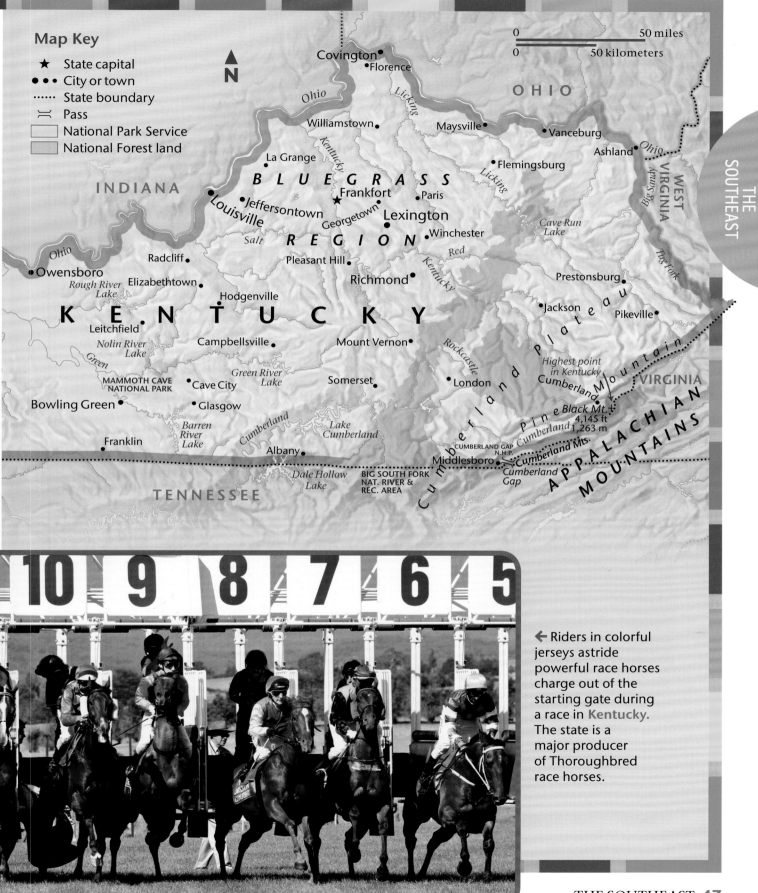

Map Key

★ State capital
••• City or town
····· State boundary
⋈ Pass
▭ National Park Service
▭ National Forest land

N

0 ___ 50 miles
0 ___ 50 kilometers

OHIO

Covington
Florence
Williamstown
Maysville
Vanceburg
Ashland
Flemingsburg

Ohio
Licking
Kentucky
Licking

WEST VIRGINIA

Ohio
Big Sandy

THE SOUTHEAST

La Grange

B L U E G R A S S

Frankfort
Paris
Jeffersontown
Louisville
Georgetown
Lexington
Winchester

Cave Run Lake

R E G I O N

Salt

Pleasant Hill
Radcliff
Richmond
Prestonsburg

INDIANA

Red
Kentucky

Jackson
Pikeville

Owensboro
Rough River Lake
Elizabethtown
Hodgenville

K E N T U C K Y

Leitchfield
Nolin River Lake
Campbellsville
Mount Vernon

Rockcastle

Cumberland Plateau

Highest point in Kentucky
Cumberland

Mountain

VIRGINIA

Green

MAMMOTH CAVE NATIONAL PARK
Cave City
Somerset
London
Cumberland
Pine • Black Mt.
4,145 ft
1,263 m

A P P A L A C H I A N

Bowling Green
Glasgow
Green River Lake

Barren River Lake
Cumberland
Lake Cumberland
Cumberland Mts.
CUMBERLAND GAP N.H.P.

M O U N T A I N S

Franklin
Albany
Middlesboro
Cumberland Gap

Dale Hollow Lake
BIG SOUTH FORK NAT. RIVER & REC. AREA

TENNESSEE

10 9 8 7 6 5

← Riders in colorful jerseys astride powerful race horses charge out of the starting gate during a race in **Kentucky**. The state is a major producer of Thoroughbred race horses.

Louisiana

 Land & Water Driskill Mountain, Lake Pontchartrain, and the Mississippi River are important land and water features of Louisiana.

Statehood Louisiana became the 18th state in 1812.

People & Places Louisiana's population is 4,670,724. Baton Rouge is the state capital. The largest city is New Orleans.

Fun Fact The Louisiana state capitol building in Baton Rouge is the tallest of all the state capitols. It is a limestone skyscraper that stands 450 feet (137 m) tall and has 34 stories!

↑ Musicians practice on a park bench in New Orleans as they wait for one of the city's Mardi Gras parades to begin.

↑ The *Mississippi Queen,* a paddle-wheel boat, churns up the water as it steams along the Mississippi River between Baton Rouge and New Orleans.

Louisiana State Flag

UNION JUSTICE CONFIDENCE

Magnolia *State Flower*

Brown Pelican *State Bird*

← Louisiana is a leading producer of shrimp in the United States. Most of it is harvested from the Barataria-Terrebonne estuary of the Mississippi River.

Springhill
Red
Caddo Lake
Caddo Black Bayou Preserve
Bossier City
Shreveport
Lake Bistineau
Mansfield
Red
Toledo Bend Reservoir
Natchitoches
Many
Leesville
De Ridder
Sabine
Lake Charles
TEXAS
Calcasieu Lake
Sabine Lake

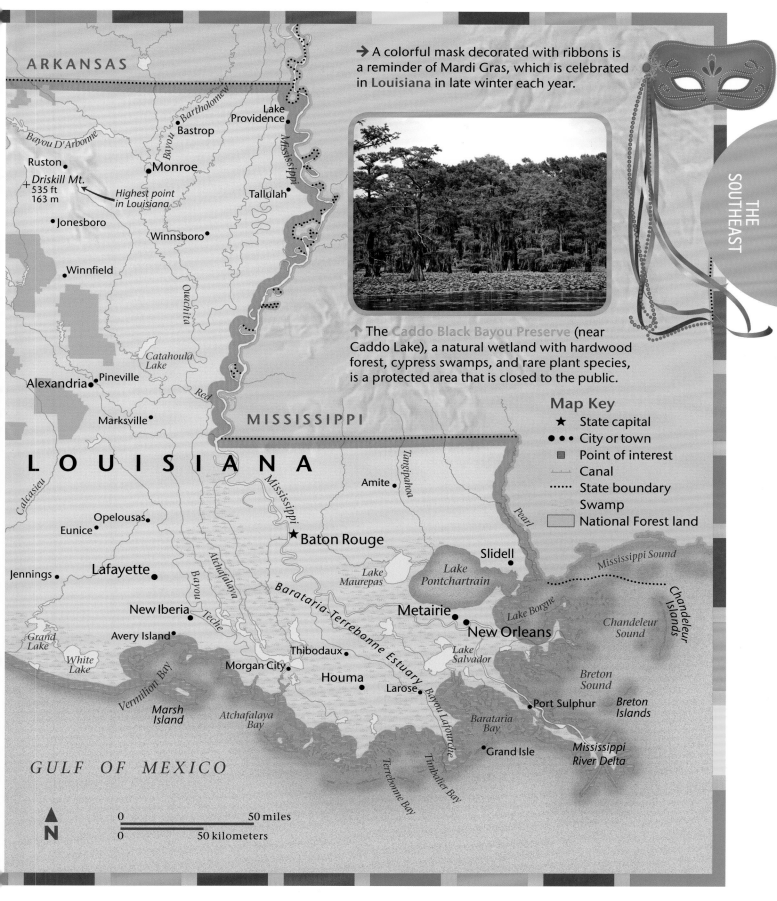

ARKANSAS

→ A colorful mask decorated with ribbons is a reminder of Mardi Gras, which is celebrated in **Louisiana** in late winter each year.

Bayou D'Arbonne

Bayou Bartholomew

Lake Providence

Bastrop

Ruston
Monroe

Driskill Mt.
535 ft
163 m
Highest point
in Louisiana

Mississippi

Tallulah

Jonesboro

Winnsboro

Winnfield

Ouachita

Catahoula Lake

Alexandria Pineville

Red

Marksville

MISSISSIPPI

L O U I S I A N A

Calcasieu

Tangipahoa

Amite

↑ The Caddo Black Bayou Preserve (near Caddo Lake), a natural wetland with hardwood forest, cypress swamps, and rare plant species, is a protected area that is closed to the public.

Map Key

★ State capital
●●● City or town
■ Point of interest
── Canal
···· State boundary
Swamp
National Forest land

Mississippi

Opelousas

Eunice

Lafayette

Jennings

★ Baton Rouge

Lake Maurepas

Lake Pontchartrain

Slidell

Pearl

Mississippi Sound

Metairie

Lake Borge

Chandeleur Islands

New Orleans

Chandeleur Sound

New Iberia

Atchafalaya

Bayou Teche

Baratria-Terrebonne Estuary

Lake Salvador

Breton Sound

Avery Island

Grand Lake

White Lake

Thibodaux

Morgan City

Houma

Larose

Bayou Lafourche

Port Sulphur

Breton Islands

Vermilion Bay

Marsh Island

Atchafalaya Bay

Baratria Bay

Timbalier Bay

Grand Isle

Mississippi River Delta

GULF OF MEXICO

Terrebonne Bay

N

0 ——— 50 miles
0 ——— 50 kilometers

↑ Mississippi is the leading producer of catfish in the United States. A part of the **Mississippi River Valley** known as the Delta is the main producing area.

Mississippi

Land & Water The Mississippi Petrified Forest, the Tennessee-Tombigbee Waterway, and the Mississippi River are important land and water features of Mississippi.

Statehood Mississippi became the 20th state in 1817.

People & Places Mississippi's population is 2,992,333. Jackson is the state capital and the largest city.

Fun Fact Jim Henson, creator of Kermit the Frog, Miss Piggy, Big Bird, and other famous Muppets, was born in Greenville.

↑ Two bridges stretch across the Mississippi River in the city of **Vicksburg.** The river is home to more than 400 species of wildlife.

↓ Children play in a tidal pool on a **Biloxi** beach as the sun sets. Barrier islands separate the city from the Gulf of Mexico.

Mississippi State Flag

Mockingbird
State Bird

Magnolia
State Flower

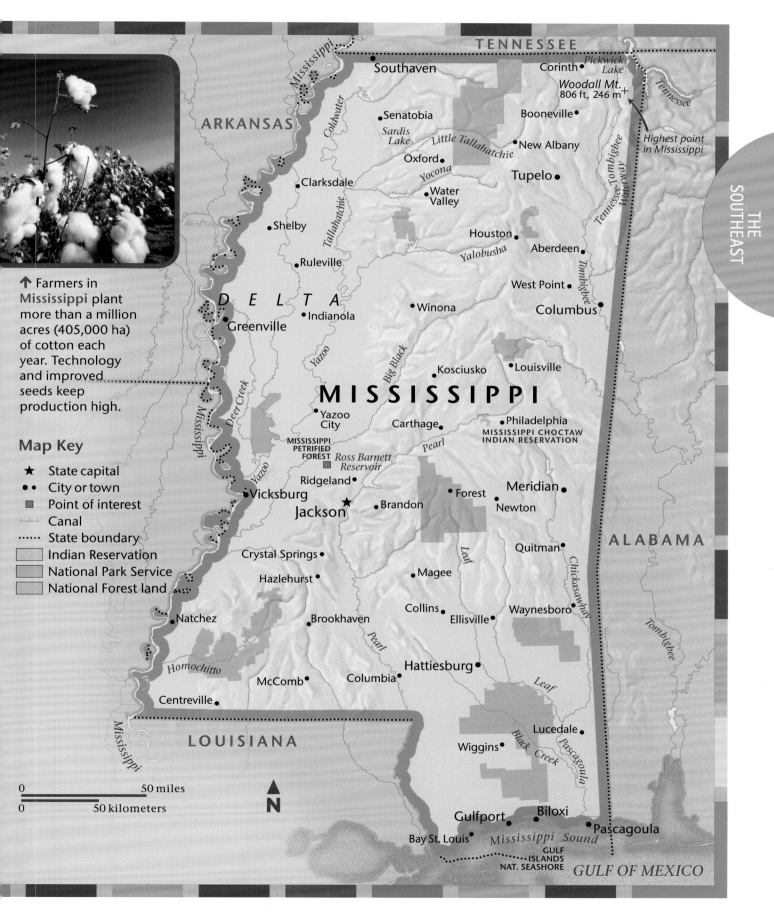

↑ Farmers in **Mississippi** plant more than a million acres (405,000 ha) of cotton each year. Technology and improved seeds keep production high.

Map Key

★ State capital
•• City or town
■ Point of interest
Canal
State boundary
Indian Reservation
National Park Service
National Forest land

TENNESSEE

ARKANSAS

Mississippi

Southaven

Corinth
Pickwick Lake

Woodall Mt.
806 ft, 246 m +

Tennessee

Senatobia

Booneville

Coldwater

Sardis Lake

Little Tallahatchie

New Albany

← Highest point in Mississippi

Oxford

Tupelo

Yocona

Clarksdale

Water Valley

Tallahatchie

Shelby

Houston

Aberdeen

Yalobusha

Ruleville

D E L T A

West Point

Tombigbee

Indianola

Winona

Columbus

Greenville

Yazoo

Big Black

Kosciusko

Louisville

M I S S I S S I P P I

Deer Creek

Yazoo City

Carthage

Philadelphia

MISSISSIPPI CHOCTAW INDIAN RESERVATION

Mississippi

MISSISSIPPI PETRIFIED FOREST

Ross Barnett Reservoir

Pearl

Ridgeland

Meridian

Forest

Newton

Yazoo

Vicksburg

Brandon

★ Jackson

Quitman

ALABAMA

Chickasawhay

Crystal Springs

Magee

Hazlehurst

Collins

Ellisville

Waynesboro

Tombigbee

Natchez

Brookhaven

Leaf

Pearl

Hattiesburg

Homochitto

McComb

Columbia

Centreville

Leaf

Lucedale

LOUISIANA

Wiggins

Black Creek

Pascagoula

Mississippi

| 0 | 50 miles |
| 0 | 50 kilometers |

▲ N

Gulfport

Biloxi

Pascagoula

Bay St. Louis

Mississippi Sound

GULF ISLANDS NAT. SEASHORE

GULF OF MEXICO

North Carolina

Land & Water Mount Mitchell, Lake Norman, and the Cape Fear River are important land and water features of North Carolina.

Statehood North Carolina became the 12th state in 1789.

People & Places North Carolina's population is 10,042,802. Raleigh is the state capital. The largest city is Charlotte.

Fun Fact The University of North Carolina, the first public university in the United States, opened its doors in 1795 with 2 professors and 41 students.

0 — 50 miles
0 — 50 kilometers

TENNESSEE

Highest point in North Carolina and east of the Mississippi

APPALACHIAN MOUNTAIN

•Boone

Mt. Mitchell
6,684 ft
2,037 m

Catawba

Hickory•

GREAT SMOKY MOUNTAINS NATIONAL PARK

Great Smoky Mts.

•Asheville

Fontana L.

EASTERN CHEROKEE I.R.

Blue

•Franklin

Chattooga

GEORGIA

SOUTH

North Carolina State Flag

MAY 20th 1775
N ★ C
APRIL 12th 1775

North Carolina State Flag

Cardinal
State Bird

Flowering Dogwood
State Flower

↑ The chapel tower is a landmark on the campus of Duke University in Durham.

← Basketball is a popular sport among all ages in North Carolina, whether on the court or in the backyard.

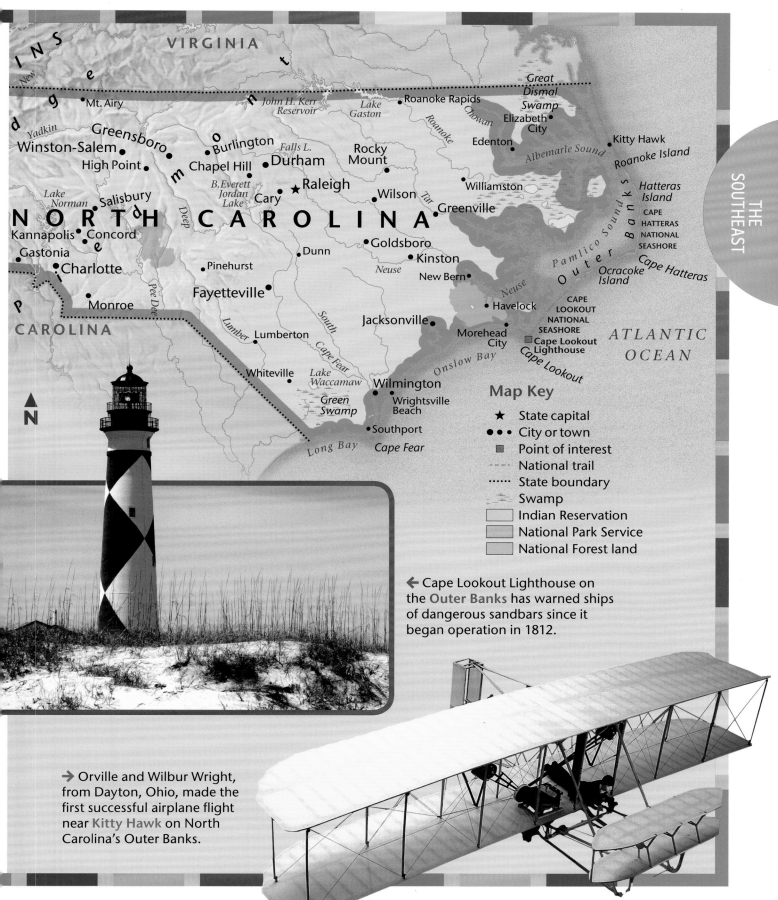

VIRGINIA

Mt. Airy

New

Yadkin

Greensboro

Winston-Salem

High Point

Chapel Hill

Burlington

Falls L.

B. Everett Jordan Lake

Cary

Durham

★ Raleigh

Rocky Mount

John H. Kerr Reservoir

Lake Gaston

Roanoke Rapids

Roanoke

Chowan

Edenton

Elizabeth City

Great Dismal Swamp

Kitty Hawk

Roanoke Island

Albemarle Sound

Williamston

Greenville

Wilson

Tar

Hatteras Island

CAPE HATTERAS NATIONAL SEASHORE

N O R T H   C A R O L I N A

Deep

Lake Norman

Salisbury

Kannapolis   Concord

Gastonia

Charlotte

Monroe

CAROLINA

Pee Dee

Pinehurst

Fayetteville

Dunn

Goldsboro

Neuse

Kinston

New Bern

Havelock

Morehead City

CAPE LOOKOUT NATIONAL SEASHORE

Cape Lookout Lighthouse

Neuse

Pamlico Sound

Outer Banks

Ocracoke Island

Cape Hatteras

CAPE LOOKOUT NATIONAL SEASHORE

Jacksonville

Lumber

Lumberton

South

Cape Fear

Whiteville

Lake Waccamaw

Green Swamp

Wilmington

Wrightsville Beach

Southport

Cape Fear

Long Bay

Onslow Bay

Cape Lookout

ATLANTIC OCEAN

Map Key

★ State capital

••• City or town

■ Point of interest

----- National trail

······ State boundary

Swamp

Indian Reservation

National Park Service

National Forest land

N

← Cape Lookout Lighthouse on the **Outer Banks** has warned ships of dangerous sandbars since it began operation in 1812.

→ Orville and Wilbur Wright, from Dayton, Ohio, made the first successful airplane flight near **Kitty Hawk** on North Carolina's Outer Banks.

SOUTH CAROLINA

South Carolina

Land & Water Sumter National Forest, Lake Marion, and the Great Pee Dee River are important land and water features of South Carolina.

Statehood South Carolina became the 8th state in 1788.

People & Places South Carolina's population is 4,896,146. Columbia is the state capital and the largest city.

Fun Fact Sweetgrass baskets have been made in the coastal lowland region for more than 300 years. They were originally used in the planting and processing of rice.

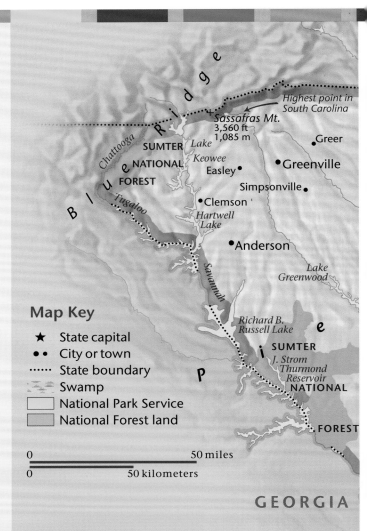

Highest point in South Carolina

Blue Ridge

Chattooga

SUMTER
NATIONAL
FOREST

Tugaloo

Savannah

Sassafras Mt.
3,560 ft
1,085 m

Lake Keowee

Easley •

Clemson •
Hartwell Lake

• Greer

• Greenville

Simpsonville •

• Anderson

Lake Greenwood

Richard B. Russell Lake

SUMTER
J. Strom Thurmond Reservoir
NATIONAL

FOREST

GEORGIA

Map Key

★ State capital
•• City or town
····· State boundary
Swamp
National Park Service
National Forest land

0 ——————— 50 miles
0 ——————— 50 kilometers

↓ Large container ships carrying valuable manufactured goods link South Carolina to the global economy. Charleston is the state's largest port.

South Carolina State Flag

Yellow Jessamine
State Flower

Carolina Wren
State Bird

NORTH CAROLINA

KINGS MOUNTAIN
N.M.P

Gaffney •

Spartanburg •

Union •

SUMTER

NATIONAL

FOREST

Wylie Lake

York •

Rock Hill •

Broad

Catawba

Lancaster •

Piedmont

Cheraw •

Great Pee Dee

Dillon •

↑ Loggerhead turtles,
which are an endangered
species, lay their eggs in
nests that they dig in the
sand of the coastal area
known as the **Lowcountry.**

*Wateree
Lake*

Winnsboro •

Newberry •

Wateree

Darlington •

Florence •

Loris •

*Lake
Murray*

Saluda

Irmo •

S O U T H

West Columbia • ★ Columbia

Sumter •

Lake City •

Black

Little Pee Dee

Plain

Myrtle Beach •

Great Pee Dee

CONGAREE
NATIONAL PARK

Congaree

C A R O L I N A

Aiken •

S. Fork Edisto

N. Fork Edisto

Orangeburg •

*Lake
Marion*

Coastal

Waccamaw

Long Bay

Williston •

Bamberg •

Edisto

*Lake
Moultrie*

Moncks Corner •

Cooper

Georgetown •

Santee

North
Island

A T L A N T I C

O C E A N

Savannah

Allendale •

Summerville •

Country

Walterboro •

North
Charleston •

Charleston •

Mount
Pleasant •

Cape Island

↓ Hard-packed sands on a **Hilton
Head Island** beach are perfect for
a family bicycle outing.

*Edisto
Island*

Beaufort •

*St. Helena
Sound*

St. Helena
Island

Parris Island

Port Royal Sound

Hilton Head
Island •

Hilton Head Island

Daufuskie Island

S E A   I S L A N D S

N

TENNESSEE

Tennessee

Land & Water The Cumberland Plateau, Reelfoot Lake, and the Tennessee River are important land and water features of Tennessee.

Statehood Tennessee became the 16th state in 1796.

People & Places Tennessee's population is 6,600,299. Nashville is the state capital. The largest city is Memphis.

Fun Fact In 1811–1812 three major earthquakes, known as the New Madrid earthquakes, changed the landscape in parts of Tennessee and Missouri. The ground in northwest Tennessee sank, creating Reelfoot Lake.

Tennessee State Flag

Iris
State Flower

Mockingbird
State Bird

➡ Memphis is famous for its barbecue, especially baby back ribs that are cooked so long that the meat falls from the bones.

⬇ Norris Dam, on a tributary of the Tennessee River, was completed in 1936. It was constructed to generate electricity.

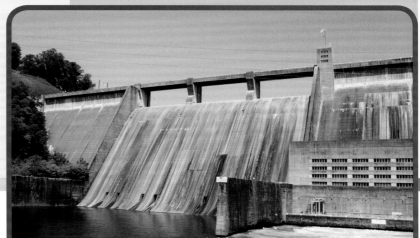

KENTUCKY

VIRGINIA

Barkley

0 ——— 50 miles

0 ——— 50 kilometers

Clarksville
Springfield
Cumberland
Old Hickory L.
Dale Hollow Lake
BIG SOUTH FORK NATIONAL RIVER AND RECREATION AREA
CUMBERLAND GAP N.H.P.
Norris Lake
Clinch
Bristol
Kingsport
Johnson City

Nashville ★
Hendersonville
Lebanon
Cumberland
Cookeville
Knoxville
Morristown
Cherokee Lake
Newport

Franklin
Smyrna
J. Percy Priest Lake
Center Hill Lake
Sparta
Oak Ridge
Sevierville
Douglas Lake

T E N N E S S E E
Duck
Columbia
Murfreesboro
Chickamauga Lake
Tennessee
Watts Bar Lake
Fort Loudoun Lake
Gatlinburg
Great Smoky Mts.
APPALACHIAN MOUNTAINS
French Broad
Nolichucky

Buffalo
Lewisburg
Shelbyville
Maryville
Tellico Lake
Clingmans Dome 6,643 ft 2,025 m
NORTH CAROLINA

Pulaski
Tims Ford Lake
Chattanooga
Athens
GREAT SMOKY MOUNTAINS NATIONAL PARK
Highest point in Tennessee

ALABAMA
Tennessee
Cleveland
Hiwassee
GEORGIA
SOUTH CAROLINA

Map Key

★ State capital
• • • City or town
- - - - National trail
· · · · · State boundary
National Park Service
National Forest land

N

↑ The Grand Ole Opry in Nashville is the home of country music. Country music performers mainly use stringed instruments. This music form evolved from traditional folk tunes of the Appalachians.

← A male white-tailed deer with a full rack of antlers watches for danger in a meadow in Great Smoky Mountains National Park. The park is a popular vacation destination.

Virginia

Land & Water
The Blue Ridge mountains, Shenandoah National Park, and the James River are important land and water features of Virginia.

Statehood
Virginia became the 10th state in 1788.

People & Places
Virginia's population is 8,382,993. Richmond is the state capital. The largest city is Virginia Beach.

Fun Fact
Eight U.S. presidents—Washington, Jefferson, Madison, Monroe, Harrison, Tyler, Taylor, and Wilson—were born in Virginia, more than in any other state.

Virginia State Flag

Flowering Dogwood
State Flower

Cardinal
State Bird

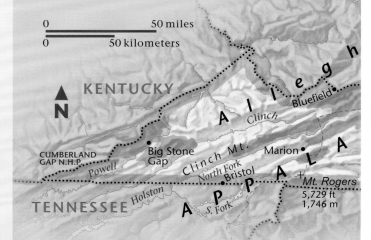

⬆ An old barn, bales of hay, and trees in autumn foliage are a common sight in the **Appalachian Mountains** of Virginia.

0   50 miles
0   50 kilometers

KENTUCKY

N

Alleghy

Clinch

Bluefield

CUMBERLAND GAP N.H.P.

Powell

Big Stone Gap

Clinch Mt.

North Fork

Marion

Bristol

APPALA

Mt. Rogers
5,729 ft
1,746 m

TENNESSEE

Holston

S. Fork

⬇ A fife and drum band maintains the tradition of military music as it marches down a street in **Williamsburg**, an early capital of Virginia.

Map Key

★ State capital
●●● City or town
◼ Point of interest
--- National trail
···· State boundary
≈ Swamp
▭ National Park Service
▭ National Forest land

MARYLAND

NEW JERSEY

DELAWARE

DELMARVA PENINSULA

ASSATEAGUE ISLAND NATIONAL SEASHORE

Chincoteague

Chesapeake Bay

Potomac

HARPERS FERRY N.H.P.

Winchester

Leesburg

Reston

D.C.

Front Royal

Arlington

Manassas

Alexandria

LURAY CAVERNS

SHENANDOAH

Woodbridge

Luray

NATIONAL

Harrisonburg

PARK

Culpeper

Fredericksburg

Rappahannock

WEST VIRGINIA

Charlottesville

Lake Anna

Cowpasture

Lexington

VIRGINIA

New

James

Appalachian

Richmond

York

COLONIAL N.H.P.

Williamsburg

Cape Charles

Yorktown

Appomattox

Petersburg

James

Newport News

Hampton

Roanoke

Blacksburg

Smith Mountain Lake

Lynchburg

Norfolk

Virginia Beach

Radford

Roanoke (Staunton)

Nottoway

Portsmouth

Chesapeake

New

Highest point in Virginia

John H. Kerr Reservoir

Danville

Lake Gaston

Great Dismal Swamp

Roanoke

ATLANTIC OCEAN

NORTH CAROLINA

→ Winding under the Appalachian Mountains, **Luray Caverns** formed as water dissolved rocks, and the minerals dripped down to create stalactites and stalagmites.

← The sharp eyes of a great blue heron watch the water of a river near Richmond for a dinner of fish or frogs.

West Virginia

Land & Water
The Allegheny Mountains, Ohio River, and the New River are important land and water features of West Virginia.

Statehood
West Virginia became the 35th state in 1863.

People & Places
West Virginia's population is 1,844,128. Charleston is the state capital and the largest city.

Fun Fact
One of the oldest and largest Indian burial grounds is located in Moundsville along the Ohio River. It is more than 2,000 years old and 69 feet (21 m) high.

↑ West Virginia's rivers offer some of the best white-water rafting in the eastern United States. The **Gauley River** is called the Beast of the East.

← A coal miner's helmet recalls the history of mining in **West Virginia**. The state produced almost 12 percent of U.S. coal in 2012.

↓ Trees turn red in the **Dolly Sods Wilderness** in the Monongahela National Forest. The area is named for an early settler family.

West Virginia State Flag

Rhododendron
State Flower

Cardinal
State Bird

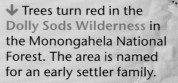

Point Pleasant

Kanawha

Ohio

Huntington

Big Sandy

Guyandotte

Tug Fork

Logan

Williamson

KENTUCKY

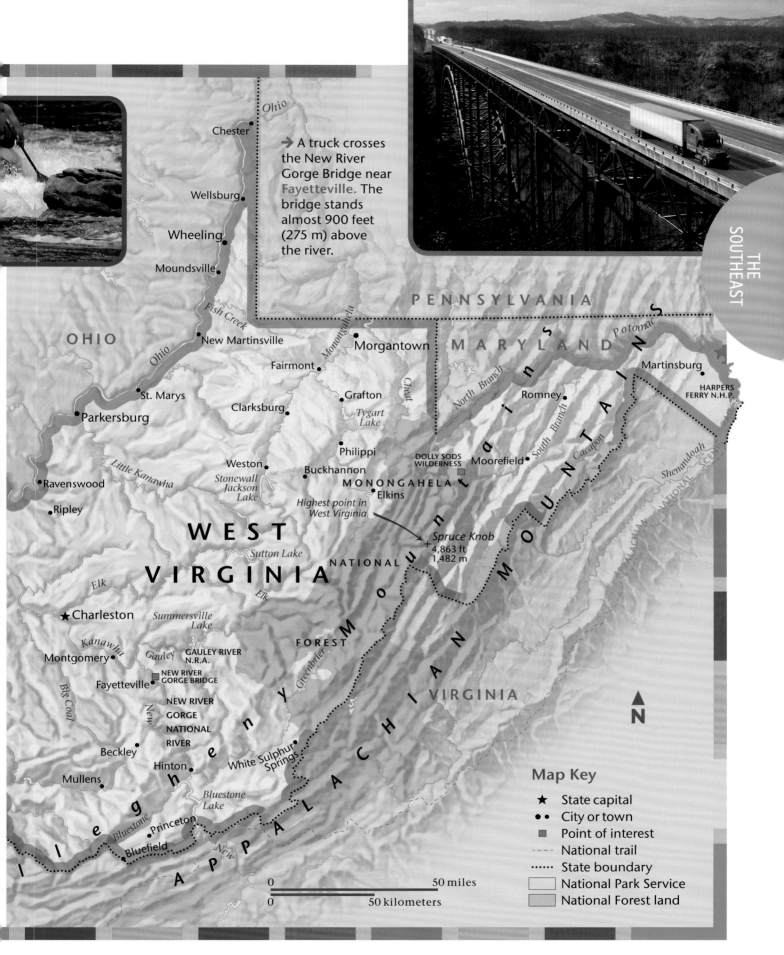

→ A truck crosses the New River Gorge Bridge near **Fayetteville**. The bridge stands almost 900 feet (275 m) above the river.

PENNSYLVANIA

MARYLAND

OHIO

Ohio

Chester

Wellsburg

Wheeling

Moundsville

Fish Creek

Ohio

New Martinsville

Morgantown

Monongahela

Fairmont

Cheat

Grafton

Tygart Lake

Clarksburg

St. Marys

Parkersburg

Little Kanawha

Weston

Philippi

Buckhannon

DOLLY SODS WILDERNESS

Moorefield

MONONGAHELA

Elkins

North Branch

South Branch

Romney

Cacapon

Martinsburg

HARPERS FERRY N.H.P.

Potomac

Shenandoah

Ravenswood

Ripley

Stonewall Jackson Lake

WEST VIRGINIA

Highest point in West Virginia

Spruce Knob
4,863 ft
1,482 m

NATIONAL

Sutton Lake

Elk

Elk

★ Charleston

Summersville Lake

FOREST

Greenbrier

VIRGINIA

Kanawha

Montgomery

Gauley

GAULEY RIVER N.R.A.

NEW RIVER GORGE BRIDGE

Fayetteville

Big Coal

New

NEW RIVER GORGE NATIONAL RIVER

Beckley

Hinton

White Sulphur Springs

Mullens

Bluestone

Bluestone Lake

Princeton

Bluefield

New

A P P A L A C H I A N   M O U N T A I N S

A l l e g h e n y   M o u n t a i n s

N

Map Key

★ State capital
•• City or town
■ Point of interest
---- National trail
...... State boundary
☐ National Park Service
☐ National Forest land

0   50 miles

0   50 kilometers

The Midwest

The Midwest is a region of glacier-carved lakes, mighty rivers, and rolling prairies. The Great Lakes are among the largest freshwater lakes in the world. The Mississippi River and its tributaries—the Missouri and the Ohio Rivers—drain America's heartland. The region's lowlands and plains support some of the most productive agriculture in the world. Industries such as food processing, steel, and automobile production supported the growth of cities such as Detroit, MI, Chicago, IL, and St. Louis, MO, but these industries are being replaced by businesses based on technology and information.

White clouds float across a blue sky above this flowering Kansas prairie. The Midwest is a major grain-producing region. Dairy cows are also an important part of the region's economy, supplying much of the country's milk, cheese, and butter.

ILLINOIS

Illinois

Land & Water

The Shawnee National Forest, the Illinois River, and Lake Michigan are important land and water features of Illinois.

Statehood
Illinois became the 21st state in 1818.

People & Places

Illinois has a population of 12,859,995. Springfield is the state capital. The largest city is Chicago.

Fun Fact
A river that runs through Chicago is dyed green on St. Patrick's Day to honor the city's large Irish population. The formula for the green dye is a closely kept secret.

← Children ride bicycles along a sidewalk in Pilsen, on Chicago's lower west side. A street mural celebrates the neighborhood's immigrant roots.

↑ Pig races are a fun-filled highlight of the annual Illinois State Fair in Springfield.

ILLINOIS

Illinois State Flag

Violet
State Flower

Cardinal
State Bird

WRIGLEY FIELD
HOME OF
CHICAGO CUBS

PIRATES 1   TOP 9TH   CUBS 4

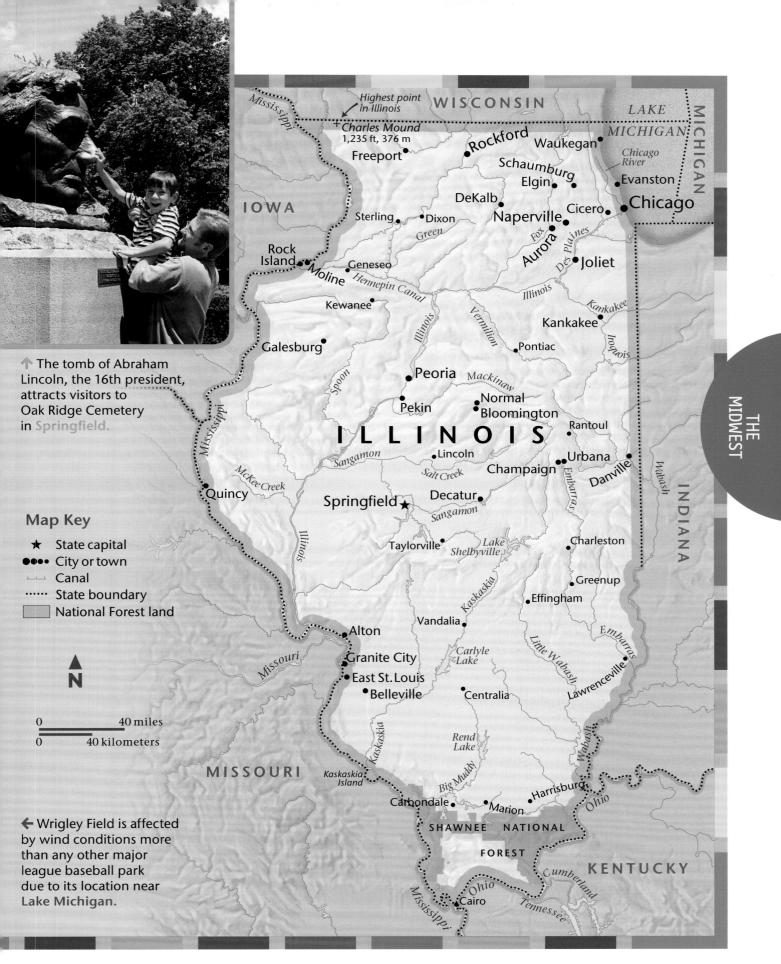

The tomb of Abraham Lincoln, the 16th president, attracts visitors to Oak Ridge Cemetery in Springfield.

Map Key

★ State capital
●●● City or town
— Canal
····· State boundary
▨ National Forest land

N

0 — 40 miles
0 — 40 kilometers

← Wrigley Field is affected by wind conditions more than any other major league baseball park due to its location near Lake Michigan.

Mississippi

WISCONSIN

LAKE MICHIGAN

MICHIGAN

Highest point in Illinois
✛ Charles Mound
1,235 ft, 376 m

Freeport

Rockford   Waukegan

Chicago River

Schaumburg

Elgin   Evanston

IOWA

DeKalb

Cicero   Chicago

Sterling   Dixon   Naperville

Green

Rock Island

Aurora

Fox

Des Plaines

Joliet

Moline

Geneseo

Hennepin Canal

Illinois

Kankakee

Kewanee

Vermilion

Kankakee

Galesburg

Iroquois

Illinois

Pontiac

Spoon

Peoria

Mackinaw

Pekin

Normal

Bloomington

Rantoul

I L L I N O I S

Sangamon

Lincoln

Salt Creek

Urbana

Champaign

Embarras

Danville

Wabash

Springfield ★

Decatur

Sangamon

McKee Creek

Quincy

Taylorville

Lake Shelbyville

Charleston

Illinois

Greenup

Effingham

Vandalia

Embarras

Alton

Carlyle Lake

Little Wabash

Granite City

Lawrenceville

Missouri

East St. Louis

Belleville

Centralia

Kaskaskia

Kaskaskia

Rend Lake

Wabash

MISSOURI

Kaskaskia Island

Big Muddy

Harrisburg

Ohio

Carbondale   Marion

SHAWNEE   NATIONAL

FOREST

KENTUCKY

Cumberland

Ohio

Mississippi   Cairo

Tennessee

INDIANA

INDIANA

Indiana

Land & Water The Hoosier National Forest, Lake Michigan, and the Wabash River are important land and water features of Indiana.

Statehood Indiana became the 19th state in 1816.

People & Places Indiana's population is 6,619,680. Indianapolis is the state capital and the largest city.

Fun Fact The intersection of U.S. Highway 40 and U.S. Highway 41, at Wabash Avenue and Seventh Street in Terre Haute, is called the Crossroads of America.

↑ The Indianapolis Motor Speedway is the largest sports stadium in the world. It seats 250,000 and hosts the famous Indy 500.

→ The Hoosiers of Indiana University, located in Bloomington, are a part of college football's powerful Big Ten Conference. Sports are an important tradition and a favorite pastime in Indiana.

Indiana State Flag

Peony
State Flower

Cardinal
State Bird

Map Key

★ State capital
•• City or town
⋯ State boundary
State Park
National Park Service
National Forest land

0 ———— 100 miles
0 ———— 100 kilometers

N

↓ A boy gathers sweet corn on a family farm near **Centerville**. Corn is an important food for both people and livestock.

LAKE MICHIGAN

MICHIGAN

East Chicago
Hammond
Gary
Merrillville
Portage
Valparaiso

Michigan City
INDIANA DUNES NAT. LAKESHORE
South Bend
Mishawaka

Elkhart
Goshen
Angola

Auburn

Plymouth

Warsaw

Fort Wayne

St. Joseph
Maumee

Rensselaer

Huntington

St. Marys

Kankakee

Tippecanoe

Eel

Wabash

Iroquois

Wabash

Mississinewa Lake

Kokomo
Marion

Lafayette

INDIANA

Muncie

Highest point in Indiana
White
Hoosier Hill
1,257 ft
383 m

Lebanon
Noblesville
Anderson
Carmel

Sugar Creek

New Castle
Richmond
Centerville

Sugar Creek

Indianapolis
Lawrence
Beech Grove

Plainfield
Greenwood

Connersville

Franklin
Shelbyville

Brookville Lake

Terre Haute

Cagles Mill Lake

Mill Creek

White

Big Blue

Martinsville
Lake Lemon

Eel

Sand Creek

Bloomington

Columbus

Whitewater

Great Miami

Monroe Lake

BROWN COUNTY STATE PARK

Lawrenceburg

Ohio

HOOSIER

Salt Cr.

Bedford

Muscatatuck

Vincennes
Washington

East Fork White

NATIONAL

Blue

Patoka

Jeffersonville

Ohio

Patoka Lake

FOREST

New Albany

Mount Vernon
Evansville

Ohio

ILLINOIS

Wabash

OHIO

KENTUCKY

Iowa

Land & Water
Hawkeye Point and the Missouri and Mississippi Rivers are important land and water features of Iowa.

Statehood
Iowa became the 29th state in 1846.

People & Places
Iowa's population is 3,123,899. Des Moines is the state capital and the largest city.

Fun Fact
Iowa's nickname, the Hawkeye State, comes from Chief Black Hawk, the Sauk Indian chief who started the Black Hawk War in 1832.

↑ Hogs outnumber people almost seven to one in Iowa, which produces nearly one-third of all hogs raised in the United States.

SOUTH DAKOTA

Hawkeye Point +
1,670 ft
509 m

Highest point in Iowa

• Sheldon

Big Sioux

• Le Mars

Missouri

• Sioux City

Little Sioux

• Onawa

Denison

NEBRASKA

Boyer

Harlan

• Council Bluffs

Missouri

• Glenwood

Missouri

Map Key
★ State capital
••• City or town
■ Point of interest
...... State boundary

Iowa State Flag

OUR LIBERTIES WE PRIZE AND OUR RIGHTS WE WILL MAINTAIN

IOWA

Wild Rose
State Flower

American Goldfinch
State Bird

← A young Native American boy dressed in colorful traditional clothing prepares to participate in the Annual Meskwaki Powwow near Tama.

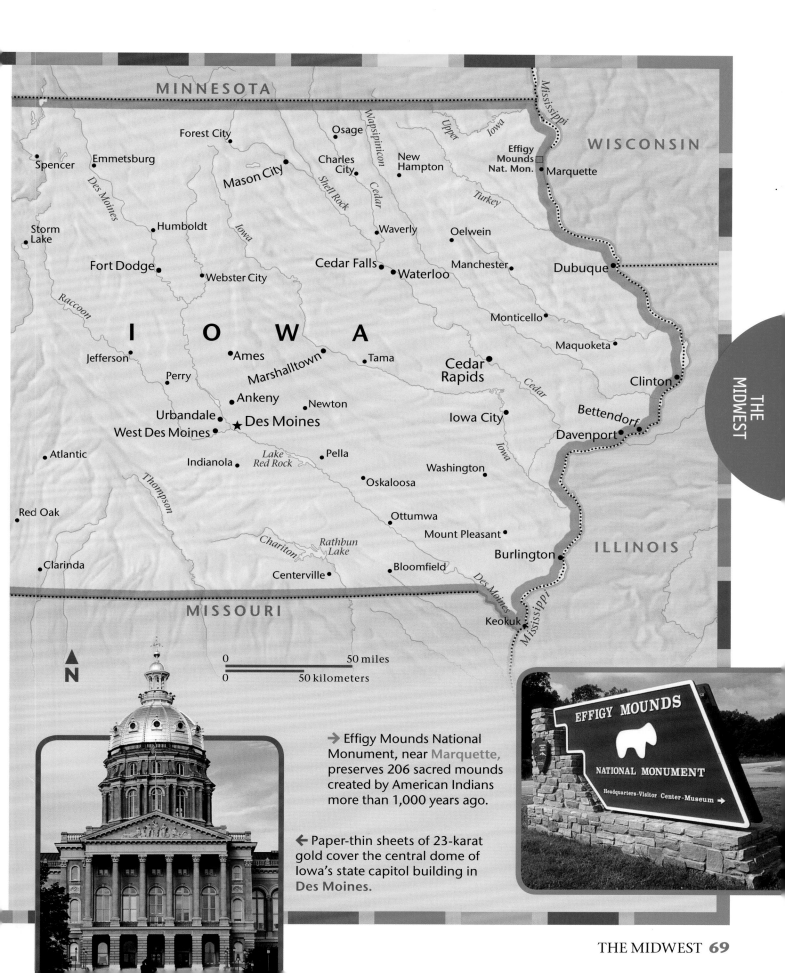

MINNESOTA

WISCONSIN

Spencer
Emmetsburg
Forest City
Osage
Charles City
New Hampton
Effigy Mounds Nat. Mon.
Marquette

Wapsipinicon

Upper

Iowa

Mississippi

Mason City

Shell Rock

Cedar

Turkey

Storm Lake
Humboldt
Waverly
Oelwein

Iowa

Des Moines

Fort Dodge
Webster City
Cedar Falls
Waterloo
Manchester
Dubuque

Raccoon

I O W A

Jefferson
Ames
Tama
Cedar Rapids
Monticello
Maquoketa

Perry
Marshalltown

Cedar

Clinton

Ankeny
Newton
Bettendorf

Urbandale
★ Des Moines
Iowa City
Davenport

West Des Moines

Iowa

Atlantic
Indianola
Lake Red Rock
Pella
Washington

Thompson

Oskaloosa

Red Oak
Ottumwa
Mount Pleasant

ILLINOIS

Chariton
Rathbun Lake

Clarinda
Bloomfield
Burlington

Centerville

Des Moines

Mississippi

MISSOURI

Keokuk

THE MIDWEST

N

| 0 | 50 miles |
| 0 | 50 kilometers |

→ Effigy Mounds National Monument, near Marquette, preserves 206 sacred mounds created by American Indians more than 1,000 years ago.

← Paper-thin sheets of 23-karat gold cover the central dome of Iowa's state capitol building in Des Moines.

EFFIGY MOUNDS
NATIONAL MONUMENT
Headquarters-Visitor Center-Museum →

KANSAS

Kansas

Land & Water Mount Sunflower, the Flint Hills, and the Missouri River are important land and water features of Kansas.

Statehood Kansas became the 34th state in 1861.

People & Places The population of Kansas is 2,911,641. Topeka is the state capital. The largest city is Wichita.

Fun Fact Pizza Hut, the world's largest pizza chain, opened its first restaurant in Wichita in 1958. Today the company has branches in more than 100 countries.

⬆ A statue of the Tin Man, a character from *The Wonderful Wizard of Oz*, the popular fantasy book partly set in Kansas, sits in a garden.

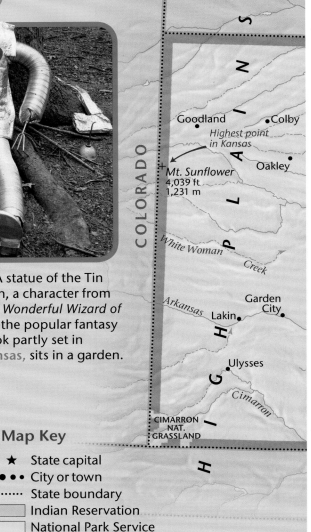

HIGH PLAINS

COLORADO

Goodland • • Colby
Highest point in Kansas
← Mt. Sunflower 4,039 ft 1,231 m
• Oakley

White Woman Creek

Arkansas • Lakin
Garden City

• Ulysses

Cimarron

CIMARRON NAT. GRASSLAND

Map Key

★ State capital
● ● ● City or town
······ State boundary
☐ Indian Reservation
☐ National Park Service
☐ National Grassland

⬇ Monument Rocks, located south of Oakley, were once part of an ancient inland sea bed. Over millions of years, erosion by wind and water has created these chalk formations.

Kansas State Flag

Sunflower
State Flower

Western Meadowlark
State Bird

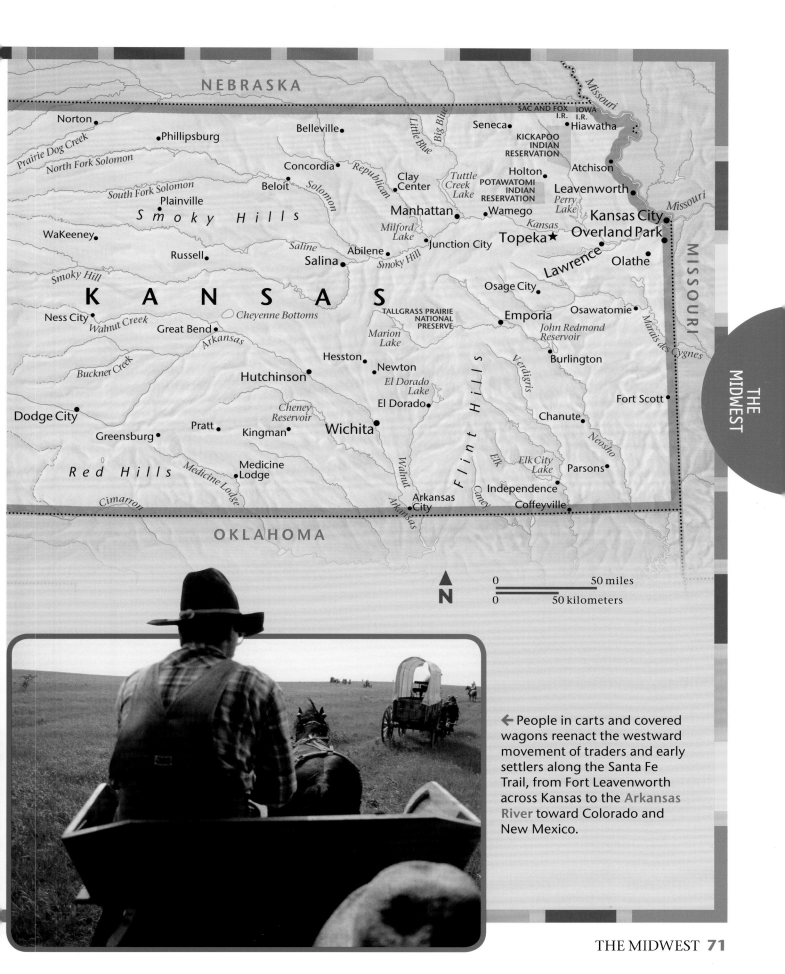

NEBRASKA

Norton
Phillipsburg
Belleville
Seneca
Hiawatha
SAC AND FOX I.R.
IOWA I.R.
Prairie Dog Creek
North Fork Solomon
Concordia
KICKAPOO INDIAN RESERVATION
Holton
Atchison
South Fork Solomon
Beloit
Clay Center
Tuttle Creek Lake
POTAWATOMI INDIAN RESERVATION
Leavenworth
Plainville
Solomon
Manhattan
Wamego
Perry Lake
Kansas City
Smoky Hills
Milford Lake
Kansas
Overland Park
WaKeeney
Saline
Abilene
Junction City
Topeka ★
Missouri
Russell
Salina
Smoky Hill
Lawrence
Olathe
Smoky Hill

K A N S A S

Ness City
Cheyenne Bottoms
Osage City
Osawatomie
Walnut Creek
Great Bend
TALLGRASS PRAIRIE NATIONAL PRESERVE
Emporia
John Redmond Reservoir
Arkansas
Marion Lake
Buckner Creek
Hesston
Newton
Burlington
Dodge City
Hutchinson
El Dorado Lake
Verdigris
Cheney Reservoir
El Dorado
Chanute
Fort Scott
Pratt
Kingman
Wichita
Flint Hills
Neosho
Greensburg
Elk
Elk City Lake
Parsons
Red Hills
Medicine Lodge
Walnut
Elk City Lake
Medicine Lodge
Cimarron
Arkansas City
Independence
Coffeyville
Arkansas
Caney

OKLAHOMA

★ N

0 ————— 50 miles
0 ————— 50 kilometers

← People in carts and covered wagons reenact the westward movement of traders and early settlers along the Santa Fe Trail, from Fort Leavenworth across Kansas to the **Arkansas River** toward Colorado and New Mexico.

MISSOURI

Marais des Cygnes

THE MIDWEST

Michigan

 Land & Water The Upper and Lower Peninsulas and Lakes Superior, Michigan, and Huron are important land and water features of Michigan.

Statehood Michigan became the 26th state in 1837.

People & Places Michigan's population is 9,922,576. Lansing is the state capital. The largest city is Detroit.

Fun Fact The record company Motown, named for Detroit's nickname Motor City, grew from a small start-up business in 1959 to one of the largest independent record companies in the world.

← A statue of Austin Blair, governor of Michigan during the Civil War, stands in front of the state capitol in Lansing.

← Boys explore nature's wonders on the bank of a river near Niles. The town sits on the site of Fort St. Joseph, built by the French in 1691.

↓ The Straits of Mackinac join Lakes Michigan and Huron. Crossing the straits, the five-mile (8-km)-long Mackinac Bridge connects Michigan's Upper Peninsula to the southern part of the state.

Michigan State Flag

Apple Blossom
State Flower

Robin
State Bird

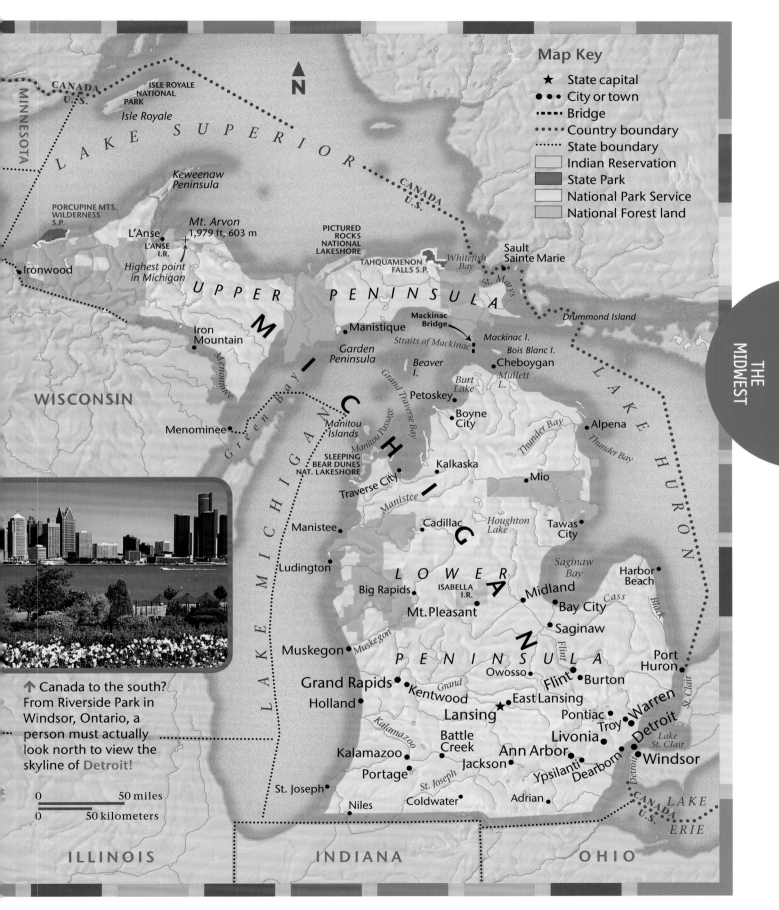

Map Key

★ State capital
●●● City or town
▪▪▪ Bridge
●●● Country boundary
•••• State boundary
☐ Indian Reservation
■ State Park
☐ National Park Service
☐ National Forest land

N

CANADA
U.S.

MINNESOTA

ISLE ROYALE
NATIONAL PARK

Isle Royale

L A K E   S U P E R I O R

CANADA
U.S.

Keweenaw
Peninsula

PORCUPINE MTS.
WILDERNESS
S.P.

L'Anse
L'ANSE
I.R.

Mt. Arvon
1,979 ft, 603 m

Highest point
in Michigan

PICTURED
ROCKS
NATIONAL
LAKESHORE

Whitefish
Bay

Sault
Sainte Marie

St. Mary's

Ironwood

TAHQUAMENON
FALLS S.P.

U P P E R   P E N I N S U L A

Drummond Island

Iron
Mountain

Manistique

Mackinac
Bridge

Straits of Mackinac

Mackinac I.
Bois Blanc I.

L A K E   H U R O N

Garden
Peninsula

Beaver
I.

Mullett
L.

Cheboygan

WISCONSIN

Menominee

Green Bay

Grand Traverse Bay

Petoskey

Burt
Lake

Boyne
City

Alpena

Menominee

Manitou
Islands

Manitou Passage

SLEEPING
BEAR DUNES
NAT. LAKESHORE

Thunder Bay

Thunder Bay

Kalkaska

Mio

Traverse City

Manistee

L O W E R

Cadillac

Houghton
Lake

Tawas
City

M I C H I G A N

Manistee

Ludington

Big Rapids

ISABELLA
I.R.

Midland

Harbor
Beach

Cass

Black

L A K E   M I C H I G A N

Mt. Pleasant

Bay City

Saginaw

P E N I N S U L A

Saginaw
Bay

Muskegon

Muskegon

Owosso

Flint

Burton

Port
Huron

St. Clair

Grand Rapids

Kentwood

Grand

Flint

Holland

East Lansing

Pontiac

Troy

Warren

Detroit

Lansing

Livonia

Kalamazoo

Battle
Creek

Ann Arbor

Dearborn

Lake
St. Clair

Kalamazoo

Jackson

Ypsilanti

Windsor

Portage

St. Joseph

Detroit

St. Joseph

Coldwater

Adrian

CANADA
U.S.

L A K E
E R I E

Niles

ILLINOIS

INDIANA

OHIO

↑ Canada to the south?
From Riverside Park in
Windsor, Ontario, a
person must actually
look north to view the
skyline of **Detroit!**

0   50 miles
0   50 kilometers

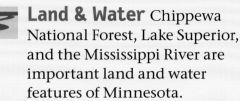

Minnesota

Land & Water Chippewa National Forest, Lake Superior, and the Mississippi River are important land and water features of Minnesota.

Statehood Minnesota became the 32nd state in 1858.

People & Places Minnesota's population is 5,489,594. St. Paul is the state capital. The largest city is Minneapolis.

Fun Fact Modern in-line skates were invented by two Minnesota students. Looking for a way to practice hockey in the summer, they replaced their skate blades with wheels.

← Minnesota's gray wolf population is growing and no longer endangered thanks to the work of the International Wolf Center in Ely.

↓ Some people in Minnesota sit for hours in "ice shacks" and fish through holes cut in the ice of frozen lakes.

Minnesota State Flag

Showy Lady's Slipper
State Flower

Common Loon
State Bird

Map Key

★ State capital
●●● City or town
▪▪▪ Country boundary
⋯⋯ State boundary

╌╌ Swamp
☐ Indian Reservation
☐ National Park Service
☐ National Forest land

The "Northwest Angle" is the northernmost point in the 48 contiguous states

RED LAKE INDIAN RES.

CANADA
U.S.

Roseau
Hallock
Baudette
Lake of the Woods
Rainy Lake
International Falls
VOYAGEURS NATIONAL PARK
Namakan Lake

Highest point in Minnesota

RED LAKE INDIAN RES.
Rainy
Big Fork

BOUNDARY WATERS

CANADA
U.S.

Thief River Falls
Red Lake
Mud Lake
RED LAKE INDIAN RESERVATION
Upper Red Lake
BOIS FORTE I.R.
Vermilion Lake
BOIS FORTE (DEER CREEK) I.R.
Ely
Eagle Mt. 2,301 ft 701 m
GRAND PORTAGE I.R.
Grand Marais

Red Lake
Source of the Mississippi River
Red Lake
Lower Red Lake
Winnibigoshish
CHIPPEWA

Mesabi Range

LAKE SUPERIOR

MICHIGAN

Wild Rice
WHITE EARTH INDIAN RESERVATION
Mississippi
Lake Itasca
Lake
NATIONAL
LEECH LAKE INDIAN RES.
FOREST
Leech Lake
Grand Rapids

Two Harbors

Park Rapids

Moorhead
Pelican Rapids
Detroit Lakes
Wadena
Crow Wing
Mississippi
Duluth
St. Louis
FOND DU LAC I.R.
Proctor
Cloquet

Brainerd
Mille Lacs Lake
Sandstone
St. Croix

MINNESOTA

Little Falls
MILLE LACS I.R.
Alexandria

ST. CROIX NATIONAL SCENIC RIVERWAY

NORTH DAKOTA

Bois de Sioux
Lake Traverse
Morris
Milaca
Rum

WISCONSIN

Chippewa
N. Fork

St. Cloud
Mississippi

Ortonville
Benson
Crow
Brooklyn Park
Coon Rapids
Stillwater

N

Litchfield
Montevideo
S. Fork
Minneapolis
★ St. Paul
Crow
Hutchinson
Eagan
Bloomington
Lakeville

SOUTH DAKOTA

Minnesota
LOWER SIOUX I.R.
Redwood Falls
Red Wing
Lake Pepin

New Ulm
Mankato

Pipestone
St. James
Rochester
Winona
Mississippi

Blue Earth
Preston
Root

Fairmont

IOWA

0 ——— 50 miles
0 ——— 50 kilometers

← The skyline of Minneapolis rises above Lake Harriet, part of a popular recreation area called Chain of Lakes.

↑ A young woman wearing the traditional dress of an Indian princess prepares to join the dancing at the Minneapolis Powwow.

MISSOURI

Missouri

Land & Water Mark Twain National Forest and the Missouri and Mississippi Rivers are important land and water features of Missouri.

Statehood Missouri became the 24th state in 1821.

People & Places Missouri's population is 6,083,672. Jefferson City is the state capital. The largest city is Kansas City.

Fun Fact Mark Twain's childhood in Hannibal, a town on the Mississippi River, inspired many of his books, including *The Adventures of Tom Sawyer* and *The Adventures of Huckleberry Finn*.

↑ In 2004 St. Charles celebrated the bicentennial of the Lewis and Clark expedition, which explored the northwestern part of the Louisiana Purchase. The historic journey began in Missouri.

← Gateway Arch, completed in 1965, recognizes the role St. Louis played in U.S. westward expansion. Trams carry one million tourists to the top of the arch each year.

Missouri State Flag

Eastern Bluebird
State Bird

Hawthorn
State Flower

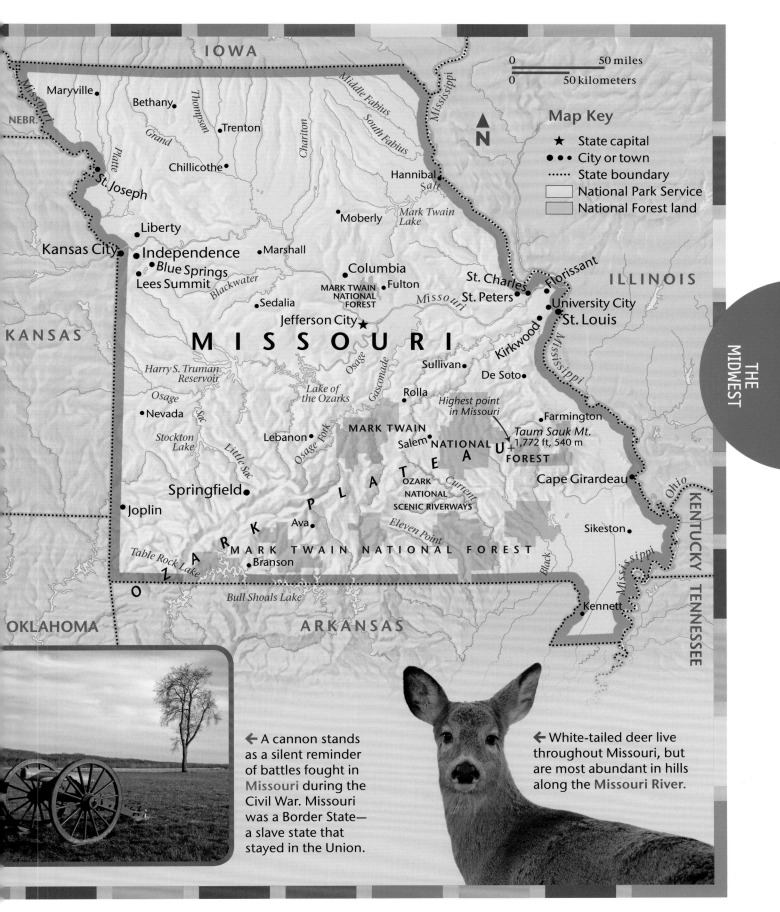

IOWA

NEBR.

Maryville

Bethany

Thompson

Trenton

Chariton

Middle Fabius

South Fabius

Mississippi

Grand

Chillicothe

Platte

St. Joseph

Liberty

Kansas City

Independence

Blue Springs

Lees Summit

Blackwater

Marshall

Sedalia

Columbia

MARK TWAIN NATIONAL FOREST

Fulton

Hannibal

Salt

Mark Twain Lake

Moberly

St. Charles

Florissant

St. Peters

University City

St. Louis

Missouri

Jefferson City ★

M I S S O U R I

KANSAS

Osage

Harry S. Truman Reservoir

Osage

Nevada

Stockton Lake

Sac

Little Sac

Lebanon

Osage York

Lake of the Ozarks

Gasconade

Rolla

Sullivan

De Soto

Kirkwood

Farmington

Highest point in Missouri

Taum Sauk Mt. 1,772 ft, 540 m

MARK TWAIN

Salem

NATIONAL

FOREST

Cape Girardeau

Springfield

Joplin

OZARK

PLATEAU

Ava

OZARK NATIONAL SCENIC RIVERWAYS

Current

Eleven Point

Black

Sikeston

MARK TWAIN NATIONAL FOREST

Table Rock Lake

Branson

Bull Shoals Lake

Kennett

OKLAHOMA

ARKANSAS

ILLINOIS

Mississippi

Ohio

KENTUCKY

TENNESSEE

Mississippi

Map Key

★ State capital

•••• City or town

...... State boundary

National Park Service

National Forest land

0 — 50 miles
0 — 50 kilometers

N

← A cannon stands as a silent reminder of battles fought in Missouri during the Civil War. Missouri was a Border State— a slave state that stayed in the Union.

← White-tailed deer live throughout Missouri, but are most abundant in hills along the Missouri River.

Nebraska

NEBRASKA

Land & Water
The Sand Hills and the Platte and Missouri Rivers are important land and water features of Nebraska.

Statehood
Nebraska became the 37th state in 1867.

People & Places
Nebraska's population is 1,896,190. Lincoln is the state capital. The largest city is Omaha.

Fun Fact
The largest remaining area of original native prairie in the United States is in the Sand Hills region. It is an important stopover for migrating sandhill cranes.

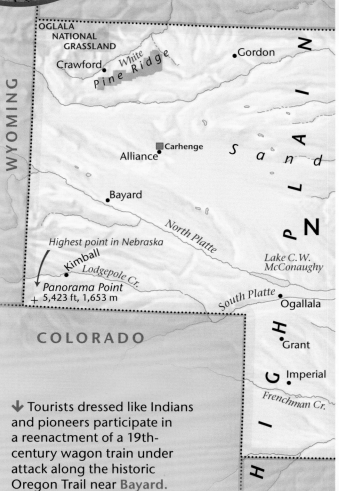

← Two black-tailed prairie dogs watch for signs of danger at the entrance to their burrow in the **Fort Niobrara National Wildlife Refuge**.

OGLALA NATIONAL GRASSLAND

Crawford • White — Pine Ridge

WYOMING

• Gordon

■ Carhenge

Alliance •

S a n d

• Bayard

Highest point in Nebraska

North Platte

Kimball • Lodgepole Cr.

Panorama Point
+ 5,423 ft, 1,653 m

COLORADO

P L A I N S

H I G H

Lake C.W. McConaughy

South Platte

• Ogallala

• Grant

• Imperial

Frenchman Cr.

↓ Tourists dressed like Indians and pioneers participate in a reenactment of a 19th-century wagon train under attack along the historic Oregon Trail near **Bayard**.

Nebraska State Flag

Goldenrod
State Flower

Western Meadowlark
State Bird

Map Key

★ State capital
●●● City or town
▪ Point of interest
····· State boundary

☐ Indian Reservation
☐ National Forest land
☐ National Grassland
☐ National Wildlife Reserve

SOUTH DAKOTA

Missouri
Lewis and
Clark Lake

Valentine
Niobrara
FORT
NIOBRARA
N.W.R.

Niobrara

SANTEE
INDIAN
RES.
Hartington

Atkinson

Logan Creek

South
Sioux City

WINNEBAGO
I.R.

OMAHA
I.R.

Gordon Cr.

H i l l s
Mullen

North Loup

Middle Loup

Elkhorn

Norfolk

Tekamah

IOWA

N E B R A S K A

Burwell

South Loup

Broken
Bow

Columbus

Loup

Fremont

Omaha

Bellevue

Wahoo

Platte

Plattsmouth

North Platte

Ravenna

St. Paul

Big Blue

Platte
Gothenburg

Grand
Island

York

★ Lincoln

Nebraska
City

Red Willow Creek

Kearney

Hastings

Crete

MISSOURI

Holdrege

Minden

Geneva

Auburn

Missouri

McCook

Republican

Alma

Little Blue

Red Cloud

Superior

Fairbury

Big Nemaha

SAC AND FOX I.R. IOWA
I.R.

KANSAS

↑ In recent years
annual snowfall in
Lincoln has averaged
about 25 inches
(64 cm), creating
work for adults but
fun for kids.

N
0   50 miles
0   50 kilometers

→ Carhenge, near **Alliance**,
is a sculpture made out of
old cars that are painted
gray and designed to look
like Stonehenge, which is a
famous archaeological site
in southern England.

NORTH DAKOTA

North Dakota

⬆ Fossils of prehistoric life, such as this leaf, can be found in **North Dakota**'s sedimentary rock formations.

⚡ **Land & Water** The Badlands, the Red River of the North, and the Missouri River are important land and water features of North Dakota.

🚩 **Statehood** North Dakota became the 39th state in 1889.

👤 **People & Places** North Dakota's population is 756,927. Bismarck is the state capital. The largest city is Fargo.

❓ **Fun Fact** North Dakota leads the United States in honey production, with more than 33 million pounds (14 million kg) produced annually. In addition to honey, bees produce wax and help pollinate crops.

⬆ Cowboys on the fence watch the excitement of the rodeo during the Slope County Fair in **Amidon**.

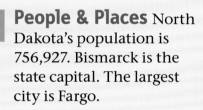

North Dakota State Flag

Wild Prairie Rose
State Flower

Western Meadowlark
State Bird

CANADA
U.S.

MONTANA

Williston

Missouri

LITTLE

Watford City

THEODORE ROOSEVELT N.P. (NORTH UNIT)

Little Missouri

MISSOURI

Theodore Roosevelt N.P. (Elkhorn Ranch Site)

Yellowstone

B a d l a n d s

NATIONAL

Medora

THEODORE ROOSEVELT N.P. (SOUTH UNIT)

GRASSLAND

Amidon

+ *White Butte*
3,506 ft
1,069 m

Highest point in North Dakota

Little Missouri

Cedar

Hettinger

0   100 miles
0   100 kilometers

N

⬅ American bison are native to the Great Plains, but now they are found mainly in parks such as **Sullys Hill National Game Preserve**.

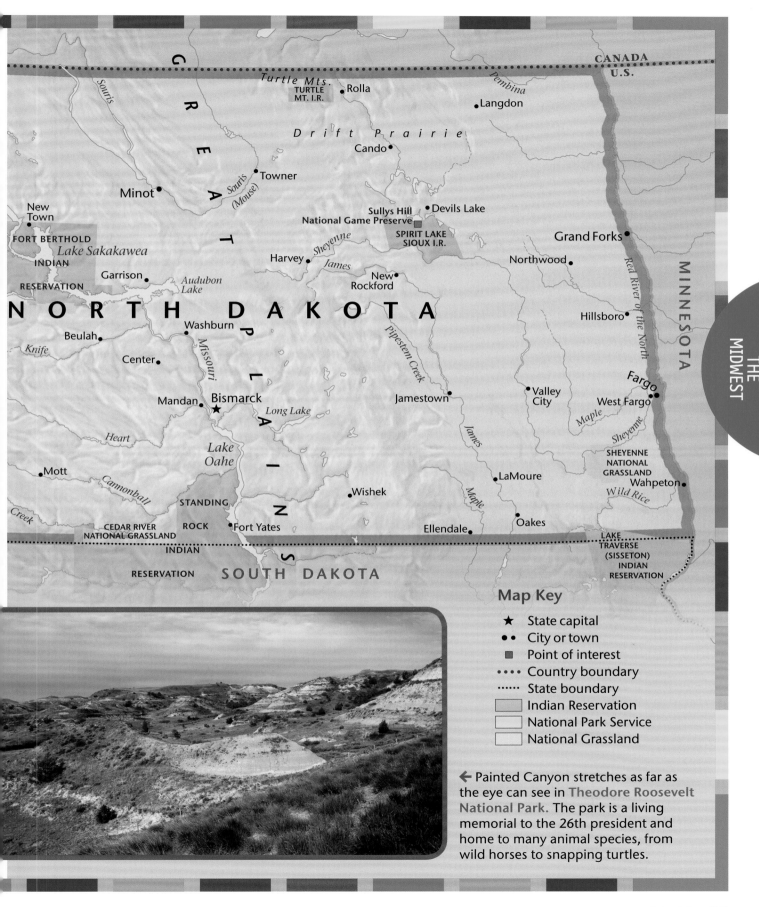

CANADA
U.S.

GREAT

Souris

Turtle Mts.
TURTLE
MT. I.R.

Rolla

Langdon

Pembina

Drift Prairie

Cando

Minot

Souris
(Mouse)

Towner

New
Town

Sullys Hill
National Game Preserve

Devils Lake

Grand Forks

FORT BERTHOLD

Lake Sakakawea

INDIAN

RESERVATION

Garrison

Audubon
Lake

Sheyenne

Harvey

James

New
Rockford

SPIRIT LAKE
SIOUX I.R.

Northwood

NORTH DAKOTA

Hillsboro

MINNESOTA

Beulah

Washburn

P

Knife

Center

Missouri

L

Pipestem Creek

THE
MIDWEST

Valley
City

Fargo

West Fargo

Red River of the North

Maple

Mandan

Bismarck

Long Lake

A

Jamestown

Sheyenne

Heart

I

James

SHEYENNE
NATIONAL
GRASSLAND

Lake
Oahe

N

LaMoure

Wahpeton

Mott

Cannonball

Wishek

Maple

Wild Rice

STANDING

S

Oakes

LAKE
TRAVERSE
(SISSETON)
INDIAN
RESERVATION

CEDAR RIVER
NATIONAL GRASSLAND

ROCK

Fort Yates

Ellendale

Creek

INDIAN

RESERVATION

SOUTH DAKOTA

Map Key

★ State capital
•• City or town
■ Point of interest
···· Country boundary
····· State boundary
   Indian Reservation
   National Park Service
   National Grassland

← Painted Canyon stretches as far as the eye can see in **Theodore Roosevelt National Park**. The park is a living memorial to the 26th president and home to many animal species, from wild horses to snapping turtles.

OHIO

Ohio

Land & Water Wayne National Forest, Lake Erie, and the Ohio River are important land and water features of Ohio.

Statehood Ohio became the 17th state in 1803.

People & Places Ohio's population is 11,613,423. Columbus is the state capital and the largest city.

Fun Fact Ohio's nickname, the Buckeye State, comes from a local tree. The tree's name was derived from Native Americans, who thought its seeds looked like the eye of a male deer, or buck.

↑ Fourth of July fireworks light up the nighttime sky above Columbus. The city has been the state capital since 1816.

↑ Colorful guitars mark the entrance to the Rock and Roll Hall of Fame, established in downtown Cleveland in 1995.

↓ The Blue Streak is the oldest operating roller coaster at Cedar Point Amusement Park in Sandusky. This popular ride is named after a local high school sports team.

Ohio State Flag

Scarlet Carnation
State Flower

Cardinal
State Bird

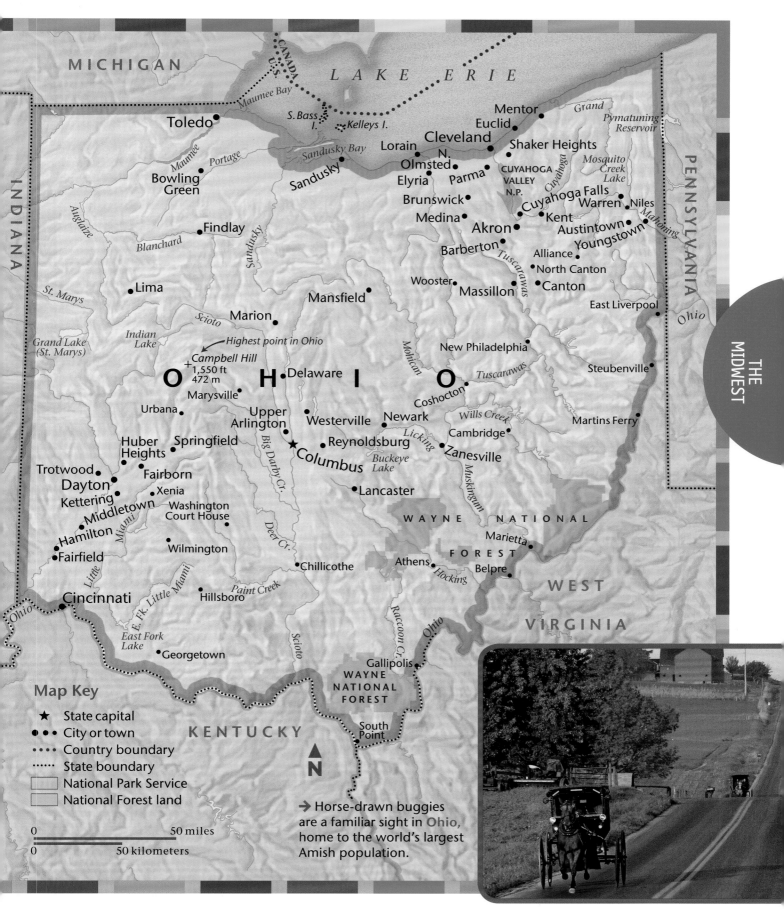

MICHIGAN

CANADA
U.S.

LAKE ERIE

Toledo

Maumee Bay
S. Bass I.
Kelleys I.

Mentor
Euclid
Cleveland
Shaker Heights

Grand

Pymatuning Reservoir

Maumee
Portage

Sandusky Bay

Lorain
N.

Olmsted
Parma

CUYAHOGA
VALLEY
N.P.

Cuyahoga

Mosquito Creek Lake

PENNSYLVANIA

Bowling
Green

Sandusky

Elyria

Brunswick

Cuyahoga Falls
Warren
Niles

Findlay

Blanchard

Auglaize

Sandusky

Medina

Akron
Barberton

Kent
Austintown
Youngstown

Tuscarawas

Alliance
North Canton

Mahoning

Lima

Wooster
Massillon
Canton

East Liverpool

Ohio

St. Marys

Scioto

Marion

Mansfield

Indian Lake

Highest point in Ohio
+ Campbell Hill
1,550 ft
472 m

O H I O

Delaware

Mohican

New Philadelphia

Tuscarawas

Steubenville

Grand Lake (St. Marys)

Marysville

Urbana

Upper
Arlington

Westerville

Newark

Coshocton

Wills Creek

Martins Ferry

Cambridge

Licking

Huber
Heights

Springfield

Reynoldsville

Zanesville

Muskingum

Trotwood

Fairborn

Big Darby Cr.

★ Columbus

Buckeye Lake

Dayton
Kettering

Xenia

Washington
Court House

Lancaster

Middletown

Miami

Deer Cr.

W A Y N E   N A T I O N A L

Hamilton

Wilmington

Marietta

Fairfield

Little

F O R E S T

Athens

Belpre

Hocking

W E S T

Cincinnati

E. Fk. Little Miami

Paint Creek

Hillsboro

Chillicothe

V I R G I N I A

Ohio

Raccoon Cr.

East Fork Lake

Georgetown

Scioto

Gallipolis

WAYNE
NATIONAL
FOREST

Map Key

★ State capital
••• City or town
•••• Country boundary
•••• State boundary
▭ National Park Service
▭ National Forest land

K E N T U C K Y

South
Point

N

0 ——————— 50 miles
0 ——————— 50 kilometers

➜ Horse-drawn buggies
are a familiar sight in **Ohio**,
home to the world's largest
Amish population.

South Dakota

↑ A mountain cotton-tail nibbles on some grass in **Wind Cave National Park.**

Land & Water The Black Hills, Buffalo Gap National Grassland, and the Missouri River are important land and water features of South Dakota.

Statehood South Dakota became the 40th state in 1889.

People & Places South Dakota's population is 858,469. Pierre is the state capital. The largest city is Sioux Falls.

Fun Fact A dinosaur nicknamed Sue was unearthed on the Cheyenne River Indian Reservation in 1990. It is the world's largest, most complete, and best preserved specimen of a *Tyrannosaurus rex.*

← Widespread dinosaur fossils in **South Dakota** prompted this humorous sign.

South Dakota State Flag

Pasqueflower *State Flower*

Ring-Necked Pheasant *State Bird*

↓ Carvings on **Mount Rushmore** in the Black Hills honor four past presidents (from left to right): George Washington, Thomas Jefferson, Theodore Roosevelt, and Abraham Lincoln.

NORTH DAKOTA

STANDING ROCK
INDIAN
RESERVATION

McIntosh

•Eureka

NAT.
GRASSLAND
•Bison

Grand

Moreau

Timber Lake•

Selby

CHEYENNE RIVER
INDIAN RESERVATION

Lake
Oahe

Ipswich•

•Aberdeen

James

•Groton

LAKE
TRAVERSE
INDIAN
RES.

Lake
Traverse

•Sisseton

Big
Stone
Lake

•Milbank

•Gettysburg

•Faulkton

•Watertown

Coteau des prairies

Big Sioux

Cherry Creek

Moreau

Cheyenne

Okobojo Creek

•Onida

Lake Poinsett

S O U T H   D A K O T A

Fort Pierre• ★ Pierre

Missouri

Bad

•Huron

•Brookings

CROW
Lake CREEK
Sharpe IND. RES.
•Fort Thompson

THE MIDWEST

Philip•

GRASSLAND

Kadoka•

FORT PIERRE
NATIONAL
GRASSLAND

LOWER
BRULE
IND. RES.

GREAT

PLAINS

•Wessington
Springs

•Madison

BADLANDS
N.P.

Kennebec•

Crow Cr.

•Chamberlain

•Mitchell

PINE RIDGE
I.R.

ROSEBUD
•White River

Little White

White

•Winner

Lake
Francis

•Platte

•Parkston

James

Sioux Falls•

RIDGE
RES.

INDIAN

Case

Martin•

RESERVATION

Keya Paha

YANKTON
INDIAN
RES.

•Wagner

Big Sioux

NEBRASKA

Lewis and Clark
Lake

Missouri

MINNESOTA

IOWA

Map Key

★ State capital
••• City or town
■ Point of interest
······ State boundary
▦ Indian Reservation
▦ State Park
▢ National Park Service
▦ National Forest land
▢ National Grassland

← Young people ride their horses past a tipi on the **Pine Ridge Indian Reservation**. The reservation is home to almost 17,000 members of the Oglala Sioux, people who are part of the Lakota Nation.

WISCONSIN

Wisconsin

Land & Water
The Door Peninsula and Lakes Superior and Michigan are important land and water features of Wisconsin.

Statehood
Wisconsin became the 30th state in 1848.

People & Places
Wisconsin's population is 5,771,337. Madison is the state capital. The largest city is Milwaukee.

Fun Fact
Laura Ingalls Wilder was born in Pepin in 1867. Her famous Little House books are based on her childhood in the forests and prairies of the Midwest.

↑ In Wisconsin bald eagles are found only in the northern regions.

← A young Native American man in colorful traditional dress dances at a festival in Milwaukee.

↑ In a winter version of sailing, ice boats compete in a race on the frozen surface of Lake Winnebago near Oshkosh.

WISCONSIN

1848

Wisconsin State Flag

Robin
State Bird

Wood Violet
State Flower

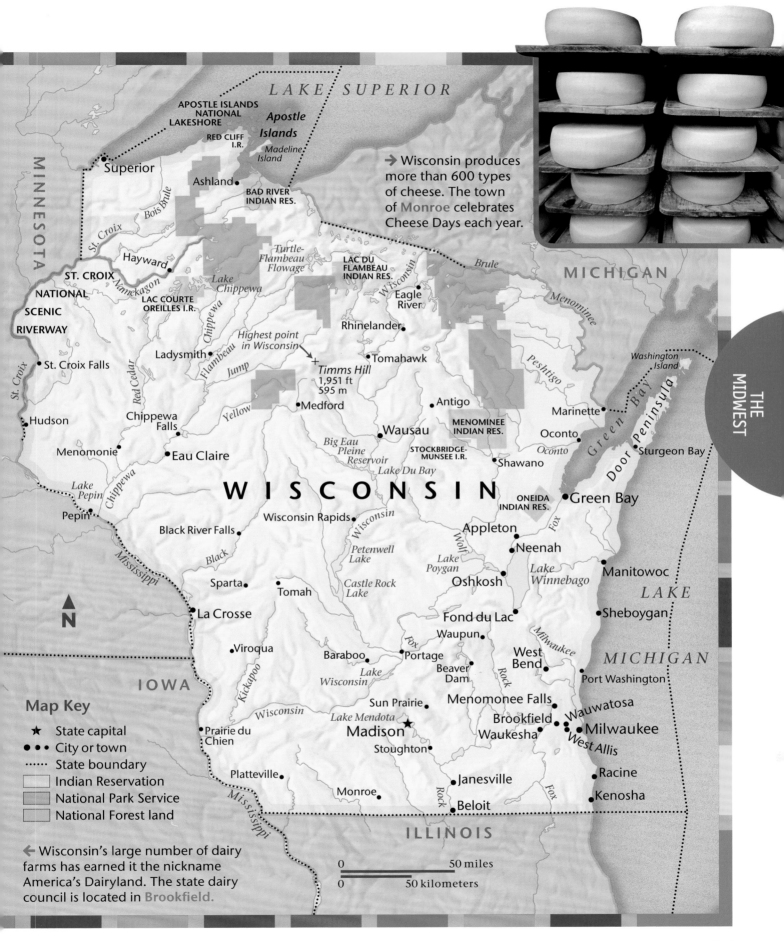

LAKE SUPERIOR

MINNESOTA

Superior

Apostle Islands

APOSTLE ISLANDS NATIONAL LAKESHORE

RED CLIFF I.R.

Madeline Island

Ashland

BAD RIVER INDIAN RES.

Hayward

Bois Brule

St. Croix

Namekagon

ST. CROIX NATIONAL SCENIC RIVERWAY

LAC COURTE OREILLES I.R.

Lake Chippewa

Turtle-Flambeau Flowage

LAC DU FLAMBEAU INDIAN RES.

Wisconsin

Brule

MICHIGAN

Menominee

Eagle River

Rhinelander

St. Croix

St. Croix Falls

Ladysmith

Chippewa

Flambeau

Jump

Highest point in Wisconsin

Timms Hill 1,951 ft 595 m

Tomahawk

Peshtigo

Washington Island

Hudson

Chippewa Falls

Yellow

Medford

Antigo

Marinette

Green Bay

Door Peninsula

THE MIDWEST

Menomonie

Eau Claire

Red Cedar

Big Eau Pleine Reservoir

Wausau

MENOMINEE INDIAN RES.

Oconto

Oconto

Sturgeon Bay

WISCONSIN

Lake Du Bay

STOCKBRIDGE-MUNSEE I.R.

Shawano

Lake Pepin

Chippewa

Pepin

Black River Falls

Wisconsin Rapids

Wisconsin

Petenwell Lake

ONEIDA INDIAN RES.

Green Bay

Appleton

Neenah

Wolf

Fox

Manitowoc

LAKE

Black

Sparta

Tomah

Castle Rock Lake

Lake Poygan

Oshkosh

Lake Winnebago

Mississippi

La Crosse

Fond du Lac

Sheboygan

Viroqua

Kickapoo

Baraboo

Portage

Fox

Waupun

Beaver Dam

Milwaukee

West Bend

MICHIGAN

Rock

Port Washington

IOWA

Lake Wisconsin

Wisconsin

Sun Prairie

Menomonee Falls

Wauwatosa

Map Key

★ State capital
••• City or town
····· State boundary
▢ Indian Reservation
▢ National Park Service
▢ National Forest land

Prairie du Chien

Lake Mendota

★ Madison

Stoughton

Brookfield

Waukesha

West Allis

Milwaukee

Platteville

Janesville

Racine

Monroe

Beloit

Rock

Fox

Kenosha

← Wisconsin's large number of dairy farms has earned it the nickname America's Dairyland. The state dairy council is located in **Brookfield.**

→ Wisconsin produces more than 600 types of cheese. The town of **Monroe** celebrates Cheese Days each year.

Mississippi

ILLINOIS

0   50 miles

0   50 kilometers

The Southwest

The Southwest region extends from the humid Gulf Coast in the east to the arid canyonlands in the west. The people of the region are just as varied as the natural landscape. Native Americans, descendants of early Spanish settlers, and recent immigrants from Mexico and Central America contribute to this region's special cultural landscape. Agriculture, cattle ranching, and the oil industry are traditional economic activities. The Southwest is part of the Sunbelt, where rapid population growth and sprawling cities are putting pressure on the region's limited water resources.

A rainbow frames Big Bend National Park's Cerro Castellon, in Texas. This eroded mount of volcanic rock rises almost 3,300 feet (1,006 m) above the desert floor. Raising horses is a part of the cultural tradition in this region.

Arizona

Land & Water
The Colorado Plateau, the Grand Canyon, and the Colorado River are important land and water features of Arizona.

Statehood
Arizona became the 48th state in 1912.

People & Places
Arizona's population is 6,828,065. Phoenix is the state capital and the largest city.

Fun Fact
Of the 21 Indian reservations in Arizona, the largest belongs to the Navajo Nation. Native peoples and the federal government own 70 percent of the state's land area.

↑ Daring boaters get soaked as they run the rapids on the fast-flowing waters of the **Colorado River** in Grand Canyon National Park.

↓ Saguaro cactus, found in the Sonoran Desert, can grow more than 30 feet (9 m) tall.

Arizona State Flag

Cactus Wren
State Bird

Saguaro
State Flower

0 — 50 miles
0 — 50 kilometers

UTAH ——— **COLORADO**

Only spot in the U.S. where the borders of four states come together

NEVADA

GLEN CANYON N.R.A.

Colorado

Lake Powell • Page

NAVAJO

FOUR CORNERS

KAIBAB I.R.

C O L O R A D O

N A T I O N

Lake Mead

GRAND CANYON- PARASHANT NAT. MON.

LAKE MEAD N.R.A.

Grand Canyon NATIONAL PARK

CANYON DE CHELLY NAT. MON.

HOPI I.R.

HAVASUPAI I.R.

• Grand Canyon

HOPI INDIAN RESERVATION

I N D I A N

Fort Defiance •

LAKE MEAD

Colorado

NATIONAL

RECREATION

HUALAPAI I.R.

P L A T E A U

Little Colorado

AREA

Highest point in Arizona

WUPATKI N.M.

R E S E R V A T I O N

FT. MOJAVE I.R.

• Kingman

Humphreys Peak ✛ 12,633 ft 3,851 m

• Flagstaff

PETRIFIED FOREST N.P.

NEW MEXICO

Holbrook •

ZUNI I.R.

Little Colorado

CALIFORNIA

Prescott •

A R I Z O N A

Colorado

COLORADO RIVER INDIAN RESERVATION

WHITE MOUNTAIN APACHE INDIAN RESERVATION

• Quartzsite

Sun City

SALT RIVER I.R.

FT. McDOWELL I.R.

Glendale • ★ Scottsdale

SAN CARLOS APACHE INDIAN RESERVATION

S O N O R A N

Phoenix • Mesa Tempe • Chandler

Globe •

GILA RIVER INDIAN RES.

Gila

GILA BEND I.R.

MARICOPA (AK-CHIN) I.R.

D E S E R T

Gila

• Casa Grande

• Safford

• Yuma

Colorado

TOHONO O'ODHAM

Ajo •

SAGUARO NAT. PARK

ORGAN PIPE CACTUS NAT. MON.

INDIAN

Tucson •

CHIRICAHUA NAT. MON.

RESERVATION

TOHONO O'ODHAM (SAN XAVIER) I.R.

U.S. MEXICO

• Tombstone

← Native American dancers perform in the Parada del Sol in Scottsdale. This monthlong celebration ends with rodeos and a grand parade.

Gulf of California

Nogales •

U.S. MEXICO

Map Key

★ State capital
• • • City or town
■ Point of interest

• • • • Country boundary
• • • • • • State boundary
▨ Dry lake

☐ Indian Reservation
☐ National Park Service
☐ National Forest land

THE SOUTHWEST

THE SOUTHWEST **91**

New Mexico

Land & Water The Sangre de Cristo Mountains, Carlsbad Caverns, and the Rio Grande are important land and water features of New Mexico.

Statehood New Mexico became the 47th state in 1912.

People & Places New Mexico's population is 2,085,109. Santa Fe is the state capital. The largest city is Albuquerque.

Fun Fact Roswell is a popular destination for people interested in UFOs. A local rancher discovered what he believed to be wreckage of a UFO in 1947.

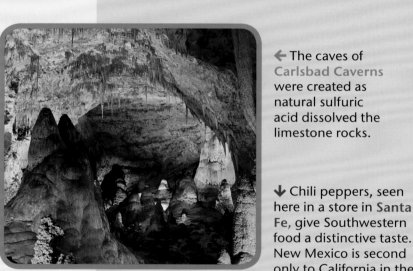

↑ Brightly colored hot-air balloons rise into a blue sky above Albuquerque during the International Balloon Fiesta, the largest such event in the world.

New Mexico State Flag

← The caves of Carlsbad Caverns were created as natural sulfuric acid dissolved the limestone rocks.

↓ Chili peppers, seen here in a store in Santa Fe, give Southwestern food a distinctive taste. New Mexico is second only to California in the production of chilies.

Yucca
State Flower

Roadrunner
State Bird

UTAH

NAVAJO

NATION

INDIAN

RESERVATION

COLORADO

Only spot in the U.S. where the borders of four states come together

UTE MOUNTAIN UTE I.R.

FOUR CORNERS

San Juan

San Juan

Shiprock

Aztec

Farmington

Navajo Reservoir

Chama

JICARILLA

APACHE

INDIAN

RESERVATION

Continental Divide

CHACO CULTURE N.H.P.

Navajo

Gallup

Zuni

ZUNI I.R.

RAMAH NAVAJO IND. RES.

EL MALPAIS N.M.

Rio San Jose

SANTA CLARA PUEBLO

Los Alamos

JEMEZ PUEBLO

ZIA PUEBLO

SANTA ANA PUEBLO

LAGUNA PUEBLO

TO'HAJIILEE NAVAJO I.R.

ACOMA PUEBLO

LAGUNA PUEBLO

Wheeler Peak 13,161 ft, 4,011 m

TAOS PUEBLO

Taos

Highest point in New Mexico

Springer

Clayton

KIOWA AND RITA BLANCA NATIONAL GRASSLANDS

ROCKY

Chimayo

NAMBE PUEBLO

BANDELIER N.M.

COCHITI PUEBLO

SANTO DOMINGO PUEBLO

SAN FELIPE PUEBLO

Bernalillo

SANDIA I.R.

Rio Rancho

Albuquerque

ISLETA PUEBLO

Santa Fe

Las Vegas

Sangre de Cristo Mts.

Canadian

Conchas Lake

Conchas

Canadian

Pecos

Ute Creek

Tucumcari

Santa Rosa

ARIZONA

Zuni

San Francisco

Reserve

Continental Divide

Gila

Silver City

Black Range

Rio Puerco

Rio Grande

ALAMO NAVAJO I.R.

PUEBLO

Los Lunas

Socorro

Mountainair

San Andres Mountains

Carrizozo

MESCALERO APACHE INDIAN RES.

Truth or Consequences

Alamogordo

WHITE SANDS N.M.

Las Cruces

Sacramento Mountains

N E W   M E X I C O

M O U N T A I N S

Roswell

Rio Hondo

Fort Sumner

Clovis

LLANO

ESTACADO

Hobbs

Guadalupe Mts.

Carlsbad

CARLSBAD CAVERNS N.P.

Pecos

Anthony

U.S. MEXICO

Sunland Park

Rio Grande

U.S. MEXICO

OKLA.

TEXAS

THE SOUTHWEST

Map Key

★ State capital
••• City or town
■ Point of interest
•••• Country boundary
······ State boundary

······ Continental Divide
  Indian Reservation
  National Park Service
  National Forest land
  National Grassland

N

0   50 miles

0   50 kilometers

Oklahoma

Land & Water Black Mesa, the Ouachita Mountains, and the Arkansas River are important land and water features of Oklahoma.

Statehood Oklahoma became the 46th state in 1907.

People & Places Oklahoma's population is 3,911,338. Oklahoma City is the state capital and the largest city.

Fun Fact Before it became a state, Oklahoma was known as Indian Territory. Today 39 Indian nations, including the Cherokee, Creek, Osage, and Choctaw, have their headquarters in the state.

COLORADO

NEW MEXICO

Cimarron

Black Mesa
4,973 ft
1,516 m
Highest point in Oklahoma

Boise City

H I G H

Beaver

Beaver

Optima Lake

KIOWA AND RITA BLANCA NAT. GRASSLAND

P L A I N S

↑ A tornado is a destructive rotating column of air that forms from a thunderstorm. In 1974 five tornadoes struck Oklahoma City in one day.

Oklahoma State Flag

OKLAHOMA

Mistletoe
State Flower

Scissor-Tailed Flycatcher
State Bird

TULSA

↑ The Golden Driller, with his hand on an oil rig, stands 76 feet (23 m) tall near the State Fairgrounds in Tulsa.

KANSAS

MISSOURI

•Buffalo

Great
Salt Plains
Lake

Salt Fork

Arkansas

OSAGE

•Miami

Lake O' The
Cherokees

Ponca
City

NATION

•Bartlesville

Vinita•

Kaw
Lake

•Pawhuska

Verdigris

Oologah
Lake

Woodward•

North Canadian

Fairview•

Rock Creek

Enid•

Sooner
Lake

INDIAN

Skiatook
Lake

Pryor•

Lake
Hudson

OZARK PLATEAU

Cimarron

RES.

Owasso•

Keystone
Lake

Stillwater•

Tulsa

Ft. Gibson
Lake

Illinois

ARKANSAS

O K L A H O M A

Edmond•

Bixby•

Broken
Arrow

Tahlequah•

BLACK KETTLE
NATIONAL
GRASSLAND

Clinton•

El Reno•

★ Oklahoma City

Deep Fork

Muskogee•
Okmulgee•

Tenkiller
Lake

Sallisaw•

Sayre•

Washita

Moore•

Shawnee•

N. Canadian

Arkansas

Robert
S. Kerr
Lake

North Fork

Norman•

Little

Seminole•

Elm Fork

Hobart•

Anadarko•

Chickasha•

Eufaula
Lake

Poteau•

Mangum•

Wichita Mts.

Purcell•

Canadian

McAlester•

Heavener•

Hollis•

Salt Fork

Lawton•

Pauls Valley•

Ada•

Sardis
Lake

Kiamichi

Ouachita Mountains

Prairie Dog Town Fork

Frederick•

Walters•

Duncan•

Sulphur•
CHICKASAW
N.R.A.

McGee Cr.
Lake

Atoka•

Broken Bow
Lake

Red

Ardmore•

Arbuckle Mts.

Washita

Hugo•

Hugo
Lake

TEXAS

Lake
Texoma

•Durant

Red

Idabel•

N

0   50 miles

0   50 kilometers

Map Key

★ State capital
• • • City or town
· · · · · State boundary
☐ Indian Reservation
☐ National Park Service
☐ National Forest land
☐ National Grassland

← Young girls wearing
traditional dress reflect the
strong Native American
heritage in **Oklahoma**.

→ The collared lizard
is Oklahoma's state
reptile. The lizard is
common in the **Wichita
Mountains** and
throughout the state.

THE
SOUTHWEST

THE SOUTHWEST **95**

TEXAS

Texas

Land & Water The Edwards Plateau, Padre Island National Seashore, and the Rio Grande are important land and water features of Texas.

Statehood Texas became the 28th state in 1845.

People & Places The population of Texas is 27,469,114. Austin is the state capital. The largest city is Houston.

Fun Fact Over the course of its history, six different national flags have flown over Texas—Spanish, French, Mexican, Texan, Confederate, and American.

Texas State Flag

Mockingbird
State Bird

Bluebonnet
State Flower

↑ The brightly lit Congress Avenue Bridge crosses Town Lake into downtown **Austin**, where tall buildings rise against the night sky.

NEW MEXICO

ROCKY

GUADALUPE MTS. N.P.

● El Paso

✛ *Guadalupe Peak*
8,749 ft
2,667 m

Highest point in Texas

U.S.
MEXICO
Rio Grande
Davis Mts.

Presidio ●

← Texas leads the United States in oil and natural gas production. A well near **Houston** pumps oil, called "black gold" because it's worth so much money.

↓ The colorful coach whip snake is found in western **Texas.** It can grow up to six feet (1.8 m) long.

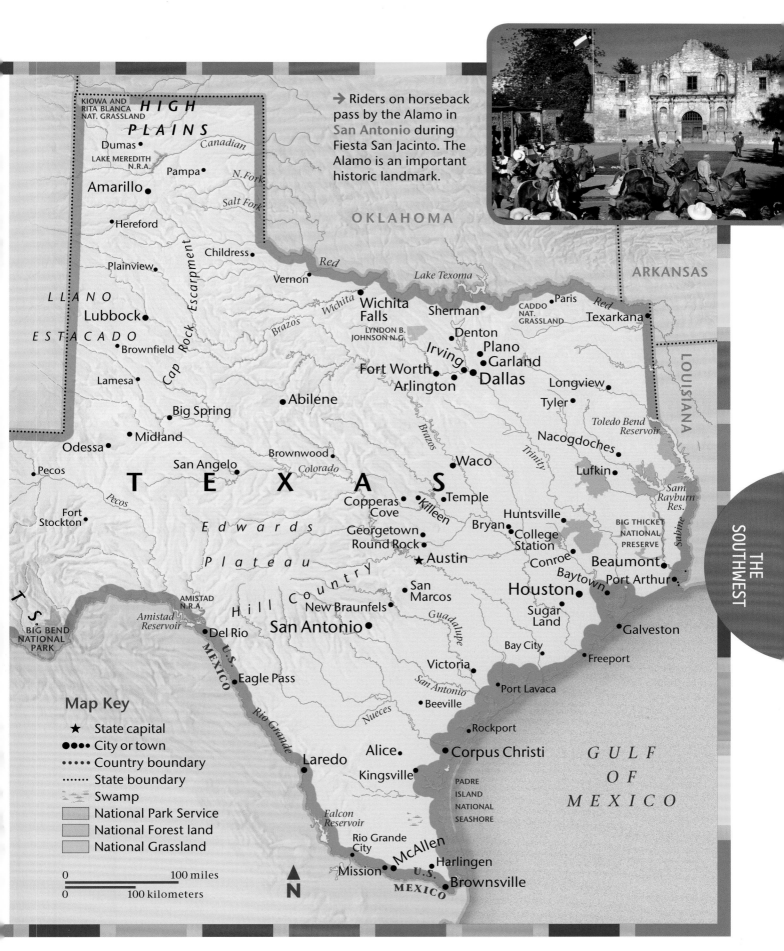

HIGH PLAINS

KIOWA AND RITA BLANCA NAT. GRASSLAND

Dumas

LAKE MEREDITH N.R.A.

Canadian

Pampa

N. Fork

Amarillo

Salt Fork

Hereford

Childress

Red

→ Riders on horseback pass by the Alamo in San Antonio during Fiesta San Jacinto. The Alamo is an important historic landmark.

OKLAHOMA

ARKANSAS

Plainview

Vernon

Lake Texoma

Wichita

Brazos

Wichita Falls

Sherman

Paris

CADDO NAT. GRASSLAND

Red

Texarkana

L L A N O

Lubbock

LYNDON B. JOHNSON N.G.

Denton

Plano

LOUISIANA

E S T A C A D O

Brownfield

Irving

Garland

Longview

Lamesa

Fort Worth

Arlington

Dallas

Tyler

Toledo Bend Reservoir

Big Spring

Abilene

Brazos

Nacogdoches

Midland

Brownwood

Waco

Lufkin

Odessa

San Angelo

Colorado

Sam Rayburn Res.

Pecos

Trinity

Temple

T E X A S

Pecos

Copperas Cove

Killeen

Huntsville

BIG THICKET NATIONAL PRESERVE

Fort Stockton

E d w a r d s

Georgetown

Bryan

College Station

Sabine

Round Rock

Conroe

Beaumont

P l a t e a u

★ Austin

Baytown

Port Arthur

Houston

H i l l

San Marcos

AMISTAD N.R.A.

C o u n t r y

New Braunfels

Sugar Land

Guadalupe

Galveston

N T S.

Amistad Reservoir

Del Rio

San Antonio

Bay City

BIG BEND NATIONAL PARK

U.S.

Freeport

MEXICO

Eagle Pass

San Antonio

Victoria

Port Lavaca

Map Key

★ State capital

•••• City or town

•••• Country boundary

•••• State boundary

Swamp

National Park Service

National Forest land

National Grassland

Rio Grande

Nueces

Beeville

Rockport

Laredo

Alice

Corpus Christi

Kingsville

G U L F

O F

M E X I C O

PADRE ISLAND NATIONAL SEASHORE

Falcon Reservoir

Rio Grande City

McAllen

Mission

Harlingen

U.S.

Brownsville

MEXICO

0 _____ 100 miles

0 _____ 100 kilometers

N

The West

The West region makes up almost half of the landmass of the United States. The region's varied landscapes and climates range from the frozen heights of Denali in Alaska, to the barren desert of Death Valley in California and the lush tropical forests of Hawai'i. More than half the population lives in California. The Los Angeles metropolitan area is second in size only to that of New York City. Other parts of the region have few people, and much of the land is set aside as parkland and military bases.

The snowy peaks of Maroon Bells–Snowmass Wilderness near Aspen, Colorado, rise over 14,000 feet (4,200 m). Mountains—the Rockies, Tetons, and Sierra Nevadas—are important landscape features of the West and provide habitat for mountain lions (right) and other wildlife.

The West

Alaska

Land & Water The Tongass National Forest, Brooks Range, and the Yukon River are important land and water features of Alaska.

Statehood Alaska became the 49th state in 1959.

People & Places Alaska's population is 738,432. Juneau is the state capital. The largest city is Anchorage.

Fun Fact The most powerful earthquake ever recorded in North America struck Anchorage in 1964. Eighty times more powerful than the 1906 San Francisco earthquake, it measured 9.2 on the Richter scale.

↑ Dogsledding has a long and colorful history in Alaska. The most famous race is the Iditarod, which runs from Anchorage to Nome along an old mail and supply route.

Alaska State Flag

Forget-Me-Not
State Flower

Willow Ptarmigan
State Bird

CHUKCHI

RUSSIA

Bering

St. Lawrence I.

St. Matthew I.

Nunivak I.

B E R I N G
S E A

St. Paul • Pribilof
Islands

A L E U T I A N   I S L A N D S   *Unimak I.*
Unalaska I.
Umnak I.   •Unalaska
Yunaska I.   Islands of Four Mountains

Continuation of the Aleutian Islands on map to the right

P A C I F I C
O C E A N

← Native peoples in Alaska carved totem poles to tell their histories. Carvers still make totem poles at Saxman Native Village in Ketchikan.

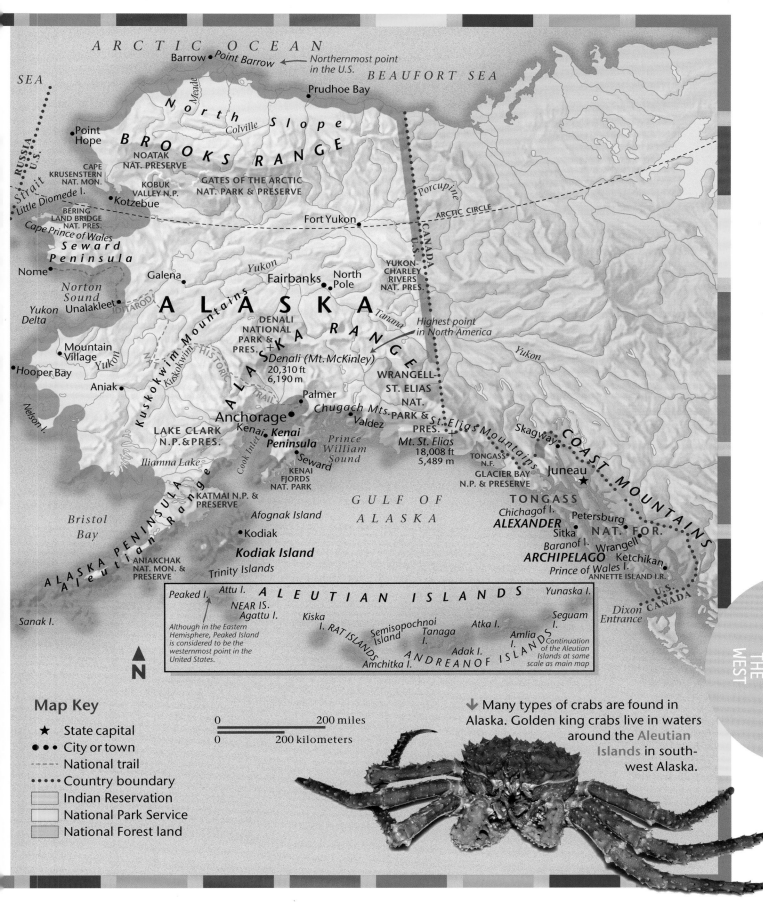

ARCTIC OCEAN

Barrow • ● Point Barrow ← Northernmost point in the U.S.

BEAUFORT SEA

SEA

● Prudhoe Bay

North Slope

Meade

RUSSIA
U.S.

● Point Hope

Colville

BROOKS RANGE

Strait

CAPE KRUSENSTERN NAT. MON.

NOATAK NAT. PRESERVE

• Little Diomede I.

KOBUK VALLEY N.P.

● Kotzebue

GATES OF THE ARCTIC NAT. PARK & PRESERVE

Cape Prince of Wales

BERING LAND BRIDGE NAT. PRES.

ARCTIC CIRCLE

Porcupine

Seward Peninsula

● Fort Yukon

CANADA
U.S.

Nome ●

Yukon

Galena ●

Fairbanks ● ● North Pole

YUKON-CHARLEY RIVERS NAT. PRES.

Norton Sound

ALASKA

Yukon Delta

Unalakleet ●

IDITAROD

Tanana

Highest point in North America

Yukon

Kuskokwim Mountains

ALASKA RANGE

● Mountain Village

Yukon

DENALI NATIONAL PARK & PRES.

● Denali (Mt.McKinley) 20,310 ft 6,190 m

● Hooper Bay

Kuskokwim

HISTORIC

● Aniak

TRAIL

Palmer ●

WRANGELL-ST. ELIAS NAT. PARK & PRES.

Nelson I.

Chugach Mts. ● Valdez

St. Elias Mountains

Skagway ●

COAST MOUNTAINS

Anchorage ●

Kenai ●

LAKE CLARK N.P.& PRES.

Kenai Peninsula

Prince William Sound

Mt. St. Elias 18,008 ft 5,489 m

TONGASS N.F.

Juneau ★

Iliamna Lake

● Seward

Cook Inlet

KENAI FJORDS NAT. PARK

GLACIER BAY N.P. & PRESERVE

TONGASS

KATMAI N.P. & PRESERVE

Bristol Bay

Afognak Island

GULF OF ALASKA

ALEXANDER

Chichagof I.

Petersburg ●

ANIAKCHAK NAT. MON. & PRESERVE

● Kodiak

Sitka ●

NAT. FOR.

ALASKA PENINSULA

Aleutian Range

Kodiak Island

Baranof I.

Wrangell ●

Trinity Islands

ARCHIPELAGO

Ketchikan ●

Sanak I.

Prince of Wales I.

ANNETTE ISLAND I.R.

Peaked I.   Attu I.

ALEUTIAN ISLANDS

Yunaska I.

U.S.
CANADA

NEAR IS.

Dixon Entrance

Agattu I.

Although in the Eastern Hemisphere, Peaked Island is considered to be the westernmost point in the United States.

Kiska

● Seguam I.

I. RAT ISLANDS

Semisopochnoi Island

Tanaga I.

Atka I.

Amlia I.

ANDREANOF ISLANDS

Adak I.

Continuation of the Aleutian Islands at same scale as main map

↑ N

Amchitka I.

Map Key

★ State capital
● ● ● City or town
--- National trail
•••• Country boundary
▭ Indian Reservation
▭ National Park Service
▭ National Forest land

0 _____ 200 miles
0 _____ 200 kilometers

⬇ Many types of crabs are found in Alaska. Golden king crabs live in waters around the **Aleutian Islands** in southwest Alaska.

The West

California

Land & Water The Sierra Nevada, Death Valley, and San Francisco Bay are important land and water features of California.

Statehood California became the 31st state in 1850.

People & Places California's population is 39,144,818. Sacramento is the state capital. The largest city is Los Angeles.

Fun Fact Death Valley is the hottest place in the United States. In July 1913 what is now Furnace Creek Ranch registered a temperature of 134°F (57°C).

California State Flag

CALIFORNIA REPUBLIC

Golden Poppy
State Flower

California Quail
State Bird

→ Stretching more than a mile (1.6 km) across the entrance to **San Francisco Bay**, the Golden Gate Bridge opened in 1937.

↑ An elephant seal on one of California's **Channel Islands** roars at a photographer who has invaded the seal's territory on the beach.

↓ In **Leggett**, automobiles can drive through the base of this redwood tree, nicknamed the Chandelier Tree because of its huge branches.

Chandelier Tree
Height 315 ft. Diameter 21 ft.
Maximum Age 2,400 yrs.
DRIVE-THRU TREE PARK. Leggett CA

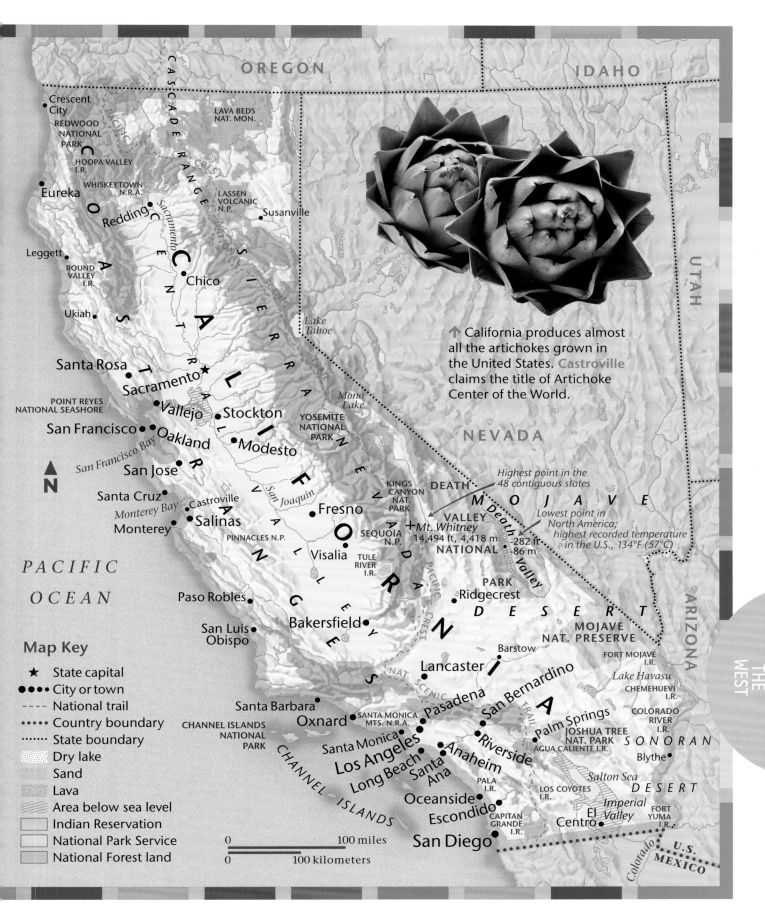

OREGON

IDAHO

Crescent City
REDWOOD NATIONAL PARK
LAVA BEDS NAT. MON.
HOOPA VALLEY I.R.
WHISKEYTOWN N.R.A.
Eureka
Redding
LASSEN VOLCANIC N.P.
Susanville
Leggett
ROUND VALLEY I.R.
Ukiah
Chico

CASCADE RANGE
CREST
Sacramento
COAST RANGE
SIERRA
Lake Tahoe
CENTRAL

Santa Rosa
Sacramento
POINT REYES NATIONAL SEASHORE
Vallejo
Stockton
San Francisco
Oakland
San Francisco Bay
San Jose
Modesto
YOSEMITE NATIONAL PARK
Mono Lake

Santa Cruz
Castroville
Monterey Bay
Salinas
Monterey
PINNACLES N.P.
San Joaquin
CALIFORNIA
Fresno
KINGS CANYON NAT. PARK
SEQUOIA N.P.
VALLEY
Visalia
TULE RIVER I.R.

California produces almost all the artichokes grown in the United States. Castroville claims the title of Artichoke Center of the World.

NEVADA

Highest point in the 48 contiguous states
DEATH
Mt. Whitney 14,494 ft, 4,418 m
VALLEY
Lowest point in North America; highest recorded temperature in the U.S., 134°F (57°C)
-282 ft -86 m
NATIONAL
M o j a v e
Death Valley

PACIFIC OCEAN

Paso Robles
San Luis Obispo
Bakersfield
NEVADA RANGE
PACIFIC CREST
PARK
Ridgecrest
DESERT
MOJAVE NAT. PRESERVE
FORT MOJAVE I.R.
Lake Havasu
CHEMEHUEVI I.R.
COLORADO RIVER I.R.

Map Key
★ State capital
•••• City or town
---- National trail
••••• Country boundary
•••••• State boundary
Dry lake
Sand
Lava
Area below sea level
Indian Reservation
National Park Service
National Forest land

NAT. SCENIC
Barstow
Lancaster
Santa Barbara
CHANNEL ISLANDS NATIONAL PARK
Oxnard
SANTA MONICA MTS. N.R.A.
Santa Monica
Los Angeles
Long Beach
Pasadena
San Bernardino
TRAIL
Palm Springs
JOSHUA TREE NAT. PARK
AGUA CALIENTE I.R.
SONORAN
Blythe
Riverside
Santa Ana
Anaheim
PALA I.R.
LOS COYOTES I.R.
Salton Sea
DESERT
Oceanside
Escondido
CAPITAN GRANDE I.R.
Imperial Valley
FORT YUMA I.R.
El Centro
San Diego

0   100 miles
0   100 kilometers

CHANNEL ISLANDS

Colorado
U.S.
MEXICO

UTAH

ARIZONA

COLORADO

Colorado

Land & Water The Rocky Mountains, Roosevelt National Forest, and the Colorado River are important land and water features of Colorado.

Statehood Colorado became the 38th state in 1876.

People & Places Colorado's population is 5,456,574. Denver is the state capital and the largest city.

Fun Fact The 700-foot (210-m)-high sand dunes in Great Sand Dunes National Park and Preserve occupy an area that was covered by an ancient sea more than a million years ago.

DINOSAUR NATIONAL MONUMENT
Green
Danforth
White
Rangely
Cathedral Bluffs
Roan Plateau
UTAH
Grand Valley
Colorado
Grand Junction
COLORADO NAT. MON.
Grand
Dolores
Uncompahgre
San Miguel
Cortez
MESA VERDE N.P.
UTE MOUNTAIN I.R.
Mancos
FOUR CORNERS
San Juan
ARIZONA
Only spot in the U.S. where the borders of four states come together

⬆ Bighorn sheep, known for their large curled horns, live in **Rocky Mountain National Park** and other mountainous areas of the West.

⬇ Early native people built more than 600 stone structures into cliff walls that are now part of **Mesa Verde National Park.**

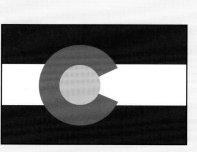

Colorado State Flag

Columbine
State Flower

Lark Bunting
State Bird

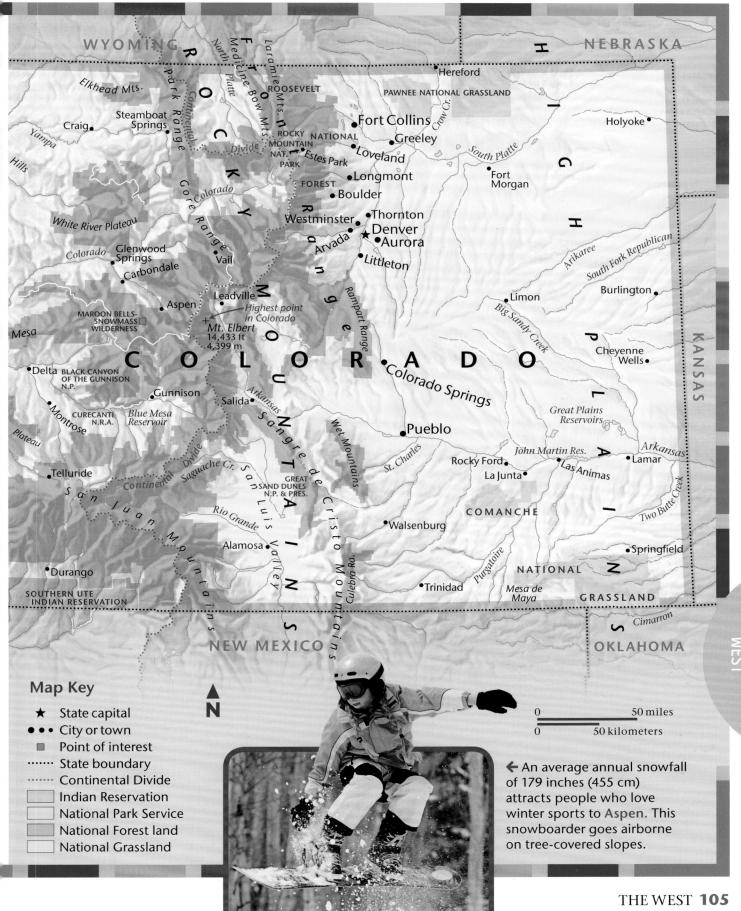

Elkhead Mts.

Craig

Steamboat Springs

Yampa Hills

White River Plateau

Colorado

Glenwood Springs

Carbondale

MAROON BELLS-
SNOWMASS
WILDERNESS

Aspen

Mesa

Delta

BLACK CANYON
OF THE GUNNISON
N.P.

Gunnison

CURECANTI
N.R.A.

Blue Mesa
Reservoir

Montrose

Plateau

San Juan Mountains

Telluride

Durango

SOUTHERN UTE
INDIAN RESERVATION

ROCKY

Park Range

Continental

Divide

Medicine Bow Mts.

North Platte

Laramie Mts.

Front Range

ROOSEVELT

NATIONAL

ROCKY
MOUNTAIN
NAT.
PARK

FOREST

Estes Park

Gore Range

Colorado

Vail

Leadville

Highest point
in Colorado

Mt. Elbert
14,433 ft
4,399 m

COLORADO

Salida

Arkansas

Saguache Cr.

Continental
Divide

Rio Grande

Alamosa

San Luis Valley

GREAT
SAND DUNES
N.P. & PRES.

Sangre de Cristo Mountains

Calabra Rd.

Fort Collins

Greeley

Loveland

Longmont

Boulder

Westminster

Arvada

Thornton

Denver

Aurora

Littleton

Rampart Range

Wet Mountains

St. Charles

Colorado Springs

Pueblo

Walsenburg

Trinidad

Purgatoire

Mesa de
Maya

Hereford

PAWNEE NATIONAL GRASSLAND

Crow Cr.

South Platte

Fort
Morgan

Holyoke

Arikaree

Big Sandy Creek

South Fork Republican

Limon

Burlington

HIGH

Cheyenne
Wells

PLAINS

Great Plains
Reservoirs

John Martin Res.

Rocky Ford

La Junta

Las Animas

COMANCHE

NATIONAL

GRASSLAND

Arkansas

Lamar

Two Butte Creek

Springfield

Cimarron

KANSAS

Map Key

★ State capital
••• City or town
■ Point of interest
······ State boundary
·········· Continental Divide
   Indian Reservation
   National Park Service
   National Forest land
   National Grassland

N

| 0 | | 50 miles |
| 0 | | 50 kilometers |

← An average annual snowfall
of 179 inches (455 cm)
attracts people who love
winter sports to **Aspen**. This
snowboarder goes airborne
on tree-covered slopes.

THE
WEST

Hawai'i

Land & Water Kilauea crater, Diamond Head, and Pearl Harbor are important land and water features of Hawai'i.

Statehood Hawai'i became the 50th state in 1959.

People & Places Hawai'i's population is 1,431,603. Honolulu is the state capital and the largest city.

Fun Fact Hawai'i is the fastest growing state in the United States—not in people, but in land. Active volcanoes are constantly creating new land as lava flows into the sea.

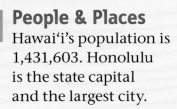

Hawai'i State Flag

Hibiscus
State Flower

Hawaiian Goose (Nene)
State Bird

← Pu'u 'Ō'ō vent on **Kilauea crater** has added more than 568 acres (230 ha) of new land to Hawai'i.

KAUA'I

Kaulakahi Channel

Wai'ale'ale
5,148 ft
1,569 m

WAIMEA CANYON

Lehua

Pu'uwai

Kekaha

Kapa'a

Lihu'e

Kalaheo

NI'IHAU

Kaua'i

P A C I F I C

↓ Hawai'i is the leading pineapple producer in the United States. Pineapples are grown on **Lāna'i, Maui,** and **O'ahu.**

Kure Atoll

Midway Islands

Pearl and Hermes Atoll

Lisianski I.

Laysan I.

Maro Reef

NORTHWESTERN HAWAIIAN

0   200 miles
0   200 kilometers

N

← A surfer balances on his board. People travel great distances to ride the big waves off the North Shore of **O'ahu**.

→ A young girl performs a traditional Polynesian hula on a misty day in Waimea Canyon on the island of **Kaua'i**.

→ Green sea turtles migrate 800 miles (1,287 km) to their nesting area in the **Northwestern Hawaiian Islands**.

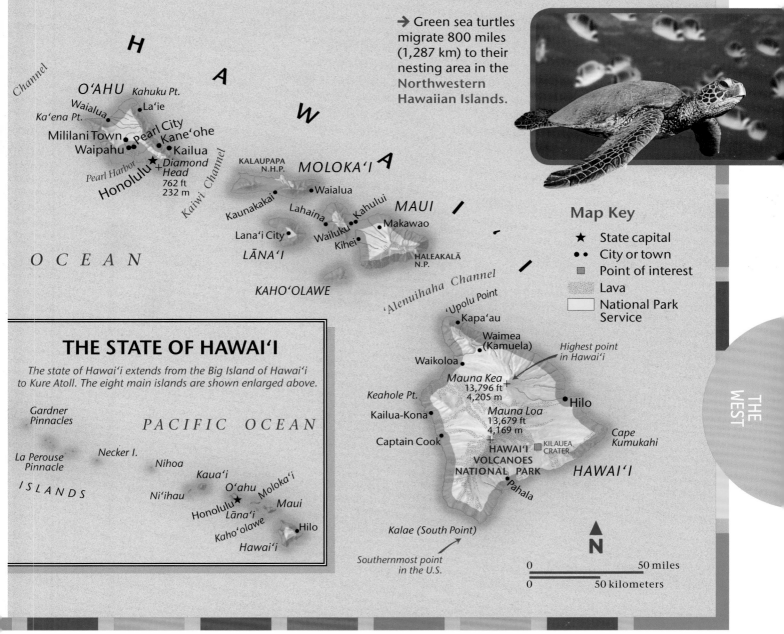

H A W A I I

Channel

O'AHU   Kahuku Pt.
Waialua   • La'ie
Ka'ena Pt. •
Mililani Town   • Pearl City
Waipahu   •   Kane'ohe
  • Kailua
Pearl Harbor   ★ Diamond Head
Honolulu   762 ft   232 m

Kaiwi Channel

KALAUPAPA N.H.P.
MOLOKA'I
• Waialua

Kaunakakai   Lahaina   Kahului
Lana'i City •   Wailuku• •Kihei **MAUI**
LĀNA'I   •Makawao
  HALEAKALĀ N.P.

KAHO'OLAWE

O C E A N

'Alenuihaha Channel

'Upolu Point
• Kapa'au
Waimea (Kamuela)
Waikoloa •
Keahole Pt.   Mauna Kea
Kailua-Kona •   13,796 ft   4,205 m
  Mauna Loa
  13,679 ft   4,169 m
Captain Cook •   ■ KILAUEA CRATER
  HAWAI'I   Cape Kumukahi
  VOLCANOES   **HAWAI'I**
  NATIONAL PARK
  •Pahala
• Hilo

Highest point in Hawai'i

Kalae (South Point)
Southernmost point in the U.S.

Map Key

★ State capital
•• City or town
■ Point of interest
  Lava
  National Park Service

THE STATE OF HAWAI'I

The state of Hawai'i extends from the Big Island of Hawai'i to Kure Atoll. The eight main islands are shown enlarged above.

Gardner Pinnacles
PACIFIC OCEAN
La Perouse Pinnacle
Necker I.
Nihoa
I S L A N D S
  Kaua'i
Ni'ihau   O'ahu   Moloka'i
Honolulu ★   Maui
Lāna'i
Kaho'olawe   •Hilo
Hawai'i

N

0   50 miles
0   50 kilometers

Idaho

↑ A wood duck perches on a post. These colorful waterfowl can be viewed in Kootenai National Wildlife Refuge near **Bonners Ferry**.

Land & Water The Bitterroot Range, the Columbia Plateau, and the Snake River are important land and water features of Idaho.

Statehood Idaho became the 43rd state in 1890.

People & Places Idaho's population is 1,654,930. Boise is the state capital and the largest city.

Fun Fact In preparation for their mission to the moon, American astronauts visited Craters of the Moon National Monument and Preserve to study its volcanic geology and experience its harsh environment.

↑ More than 40 percent of Idaho's land area is forested. Use of this land is overseen by the Forest Products Commission in **Boise**. Forest products are important to the state's economy.

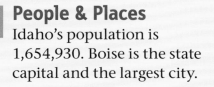

Idaho State Flag

Syringa (Mock Orange)
State Flower

Mountain Bluebird
State Bird

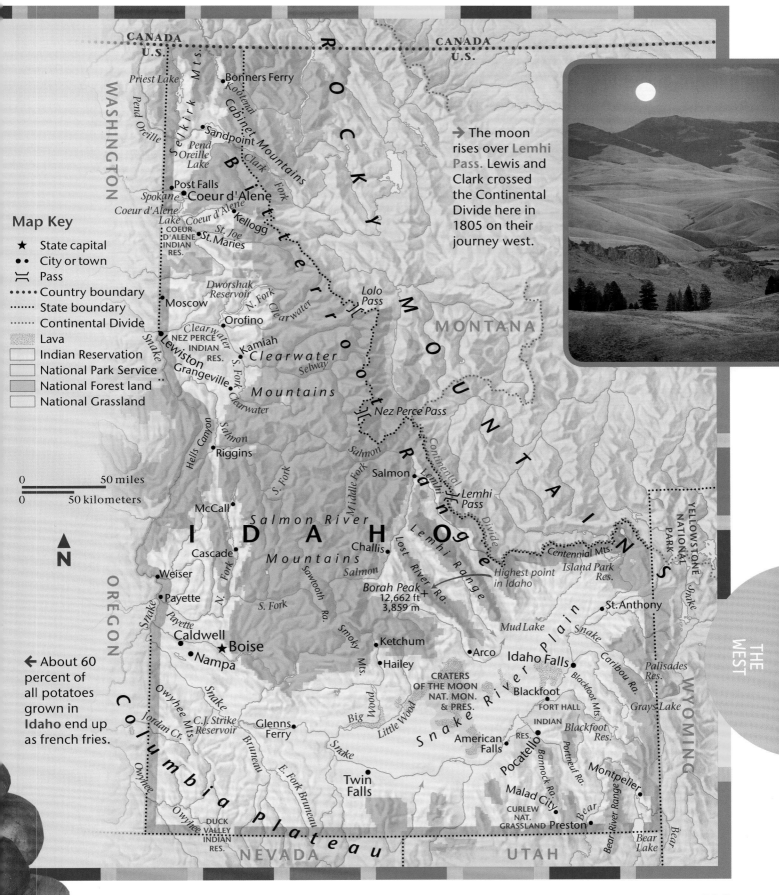

CANADA
U.S.

CANADA
U.S.

WASHINGTON

Priest Lake

Bonners Ferry

Pend Oreille

Selkirk Mts.

Kootenai

Cabinet Mountains

R O C K Y

Sandpoint

Pend Oreille Lake

Clark Fork

→ The moon rises over **Lemhi Pass.** Lewis and Clark crossed the Continental Divide here in 1805 on their journey west.

Map Key

★ State capital
•• City or town
)(Pass
•••• Country boundary
••••• State boundary
••••• Continental Divide
Lava
Indian Reservation
National Park Service
National Forest land
National Grassland

Spokane
Post Falls
Coeur d'Alene

Coeur d'Alene Lake

Coeur d'Alene

COEUR D'ALENE INDIAN RES.

Kellogg

St. Joe

St. Maries

B i t t e r r o o t

Dworshak Reservoir

N. Fork

Clearwater

Lolo Pass

M O U N T A I N S

MONTANA

Moscow

Orofino

Clearwater

NEZ PERCE INDIAN RES.

Kamiah

S. Fork

Clearwater

Selway

C l e a r w a t e r

Snake

Lewiston

Grangeville

M o u n t a i n s

Nez Perce Pass

Hells Canyon

Salmon

Riggins

S. Fork

Salmon

Middle Fork

Salmon

Salmon

Lemhi

Continental Divide

Lemhi Pass

Centennial Mts.

YELLOWSTONE NATIONAL PARK

0   50 miles
0   50 kilometers

McCall

I D A H O

Salmon River

Mountains

Challis

Lost River Ra.

L e m h i   R a n g e

Island Park Res.

Cascade

Sawtooth Ra.

Smoky Mts.

Salmon

Borah Peak +
12,662 ft
3,859 m

Highest point in Idaho

Snake

Snake River Plain

St. Anthony

Weiser

N. Fork

S. Fork

Mud Lake

Caribou Ra.

Palisades Res.

THE WEST

Payette

Payette

Ketchum

Arco

Idaho Falls

Caldwell

Snake

Hailey

Little Wood

CRATERS OF THE MOON NAT. MON. & PRES.

Blackfoot

Blackfoot Mts.

Grays Lake

★ Boise

Nampa

← About 60 percent of all potatoes grown in **Idaho** end up as french fries.

Owyhee Mts.

Jordan Cr.

C.J. Strike Reservoir

Bruneau

Big Wood

Snake

FORT HALL

INDIAN

American Falls

RES.

Pocatello

Bannock Ra.

Portneuf Ra.

Blackfoot Res.

Montpelier

Owyhee

Glenns Ferry

E. Fork Bruneau

Snake

Twin Falls

Malad City

Bear

Bear River Range

Owyhee

DUCK VALLEY INDIAN RES.

C o l u m b i a   P l a t e a u

CURLEW NAT. GRASSLAND

Preston

Bear Lake

Bear

NEVADA

UTAH

WYOMING

Montana

 Land & Water The Rocky Mountains, the Great Plains, and the Yellowstone River are important land and water features of Montana.

Statehood Montana became the 41st state in 1889.

People & Places Montana's population is 1,032,949. Helena is the state capital. The largest city is Billings.

Fun Fact Montana is the only state with river systems that empty into the Gulf of Mexico to the southeast, Hudson Bay in Canada, and the Pacific Ocean to the west.

MONTANA

Montana State Flag

Bitterroot
State Flower

Western Meadowlark
State Bird

↑ Skiers ride a chairlift up a snowy mountain slope in Whitefish.

↓ Rugged peaks of the northern Rocky Mountains are reflected in the still surface of a mountain lake in Glacier National Park.

CANADA
U.S.

CANADA
U.S.

Cut Bank

Milk

Chinook

Havre

Marias

ROCKY BOYS I.R.

FORT BELKNAP INDIAN RESERVATION

Malta

Milk

Scobey

Plentywood

FORT PECK INDIAN RESERVATION

Glasgow

Wolf Point

Missouri

Teton

Fort Benton

Missouri

Great Falls

Fort Peck Lake

Sidney

Yellowstone

Circle

Jordan

Glendive

Wibaux

Lewistown

Terry

M O N T A N A

★Helena

Canyon Ferry L.

Townsend

Roundup

Musselshell

Miles City

Baker

Missouri

Yellowstone

Forsyth

Jefferson

Madison

Gallatin

Big Timber

Billings

Colstrip

Tongue

Bozeman

Columbus

Hardin

Crow Agency

NORTHERN CHEYENNE I.R.

Powder

Broadus

Clarks Fk.

CROW INDIAN RESERVATION

Bighorn

Little Missouri

Virginia City

Granite Peak
12,799 ft
3,901 m

Highest point in Montana

Red Lodge

BIGHORN CANYON N.R.A.

Bighorn
Mountains

M O U N T A I N S

Yellowstone

West

Divide

Absaroka Range

WYOMING

GREAT PLAINS

NORTH DAKOTA

SOUTH DAKOTA

YELLOWSTONE

NATIONAL

PARK

0   50 miles
0   50 kilometers

▲
N

Map Key

★   State capital
•• City or town
⊐⊏ Pass
••••• Country boundary
•••••• State boundary
•••••• Continental Divide
☐ Indian Reservation
☐ National Park Service
☐ National Forest land

→ Many people want the experience of living on a ranch. One family-oriented ranch near Bozeman has special programs for children.

↓ American bison are protected in the National Bison Range, a wildlife refuge near Moiese.

Nevada

 Land & Water The Great Basin, the Mojave Desert, and Lake Mead are important land and water features of Nevada.

 Statehood Nevada became the 36th state in 1864.

People & Places Nevada's population is 2,890,845. Carson City is the state capital. The largest city is Las Vegas.

Fun Fact Kangaroo rats, which live in the Mojave Desert and other arid areas of the West, are small, seed-eating rodents that can survive with little or no water.

↑ The Luxor, re-creating a scene from ancient Egypt, is one of the many lavish hotels that attract millions of tourists to **Las Vegas.**

← Paiute Indians, dressed in traditional clothing, live on the Pyramid Lake Reservation near **Reno.** Their economy centers on fishing, camping, and other recreational activities.

Nevada State Flag

Mountain Bluebird
State Bird

Sagebrush
State Flower

↓ The desert environment of **Nevada** includes many plants that tolerate very dry conditions. The setting sun highlights mountains in the distance.

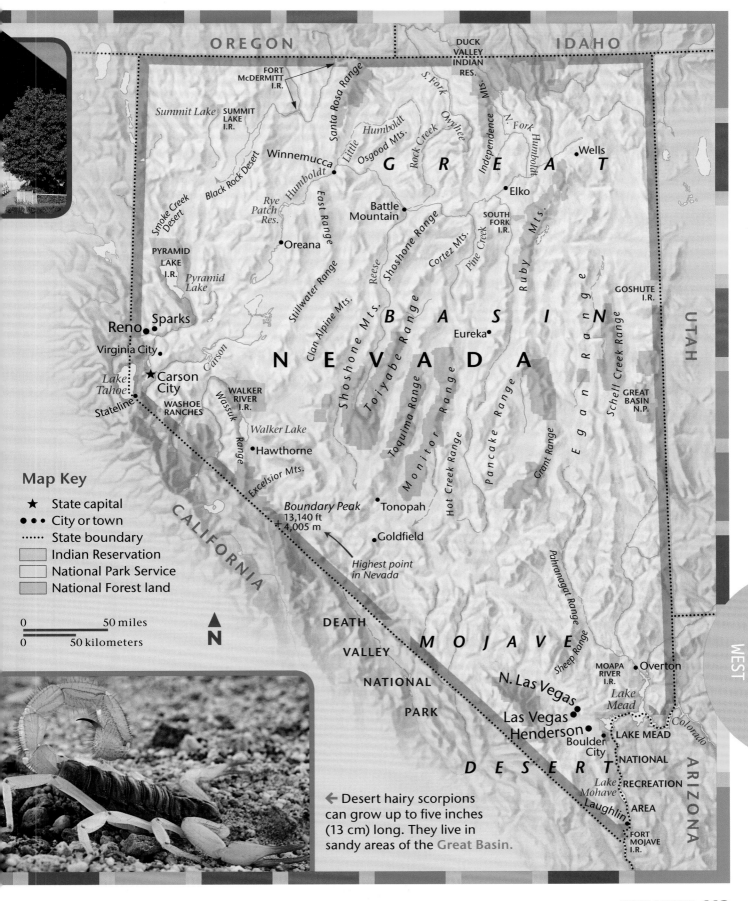

OREGON

IDAHO

DUCK VALLEY INDIAN RES.

FORT McDERMITT I.R.

Summit Lake

SUMMIT LAKE I.R.

Santa Rosa Range

Humboldt

Little

Osgood Mts.

S. Fork

Owyhee

Rock Creek

Independence Mts.

N. Fork

Humboldt

• Wells

Winnemucca

Black Rock Desert

Humboldt

G R E A T

• Elko

Smoke Creek Desert

Rye Patch Res.

East Range

Battle Mountain

Shoshone Range

Cortez Mts.

SOUTH FORK I.R.

Pine Creek

Ruby Mts.

• Oreana

PYRAMID LAKE I.R.

Pyramid Lake

Stillwater Range

Reese

B A S I N

Egan Range

GOSHUTE I.R.

UTAH

Reno • Sparks

Clan Alpine Mts.

Shoshone Mts.

N E V A D A

Eureka •

Schell Creek Range

GREAT BASIN N.P.

Virginia City •

Carson

Toiyabe Range

Toquima Range

Monitor Range

Hot Creek Range

Pancake Range

Grant Range

★ Carson City

Lake Tahoe

Stateline

WASHOE RANCHES

WALKER RIVER I.R.

Wassuk Range

Walker Lake

• Hawthorne

Excelsior Mts.

Boundary Peak
13,140 ft
4,005 m

• Tonopah

• Goldfield

Highest point in Nevada

CALIFORNIA

DEATH

VALLEY

NATIONAL

PARK

M O J A V E

Pahranagat Range

Sheep Range

MOAPA RIVER I.R.

• Overton

Lake Mead

N. Las Vegas

Las Vegas •

Henderson •

Boulder City

LAKE MEAD

NATIONAL

RECREATION

AREA

Lake Mohave

Laughlin

Colorado

ARIZONA

FORT MOJAVE I.R.

D E S E R T

Map Key

★ State capital

••• City or town

···· State boundary

▢ Indian Reservation

▢ National Park Service

▢ National Forest land

0 —— 50 miles

0 —— 50 kilometers

▲ N

← Desert hairy scorpions can grow up to five inches (13 cm) long. They live in sandy areas of the **Great Basin**.

Oregon

Land & Water The Cascade Range, Crater Lake, and the Columbia River are important land and water features of Oregon.

Statehood Oregon became the 33rd state in 1859.

People & Places Oregon's population is 4,028,977. Salem is the state capital. The largest city is Portland.

Fun Fact The Bonneville Power Administration, headquartered in Portland, provides about 30 percent of the electricity used in the Pacific Northwest. Most of this power comes from hydroelectric plants along the Columbia River.

STATE OF OREGON

1859

Oregon State Flag

Oregon Grape
State Flower

Western Meadowlark
State Bird

↑ The 125-foot (38-m) Astoria Column near the mouth of the Columbia River is covered with scenes of historic events.

↑ The cool, moist climate of the valley of the Willamette River is well suited to certain varieties of wine grapes.

↓ Rocky outcrops called sea stacks line Oregon's Pacific coast. They are the remains of a former coastline that has been eroded by waves.

Astoria

PACIFIC OCEAN

Trask
Tillamook

Newport

Umpqua

Coos Bay
North Bend
Coos Bay
Coos

Roseburg

Cape Blanco

Gold Beach
Grants Pass

Brookings
Illinois

COAST RANGES

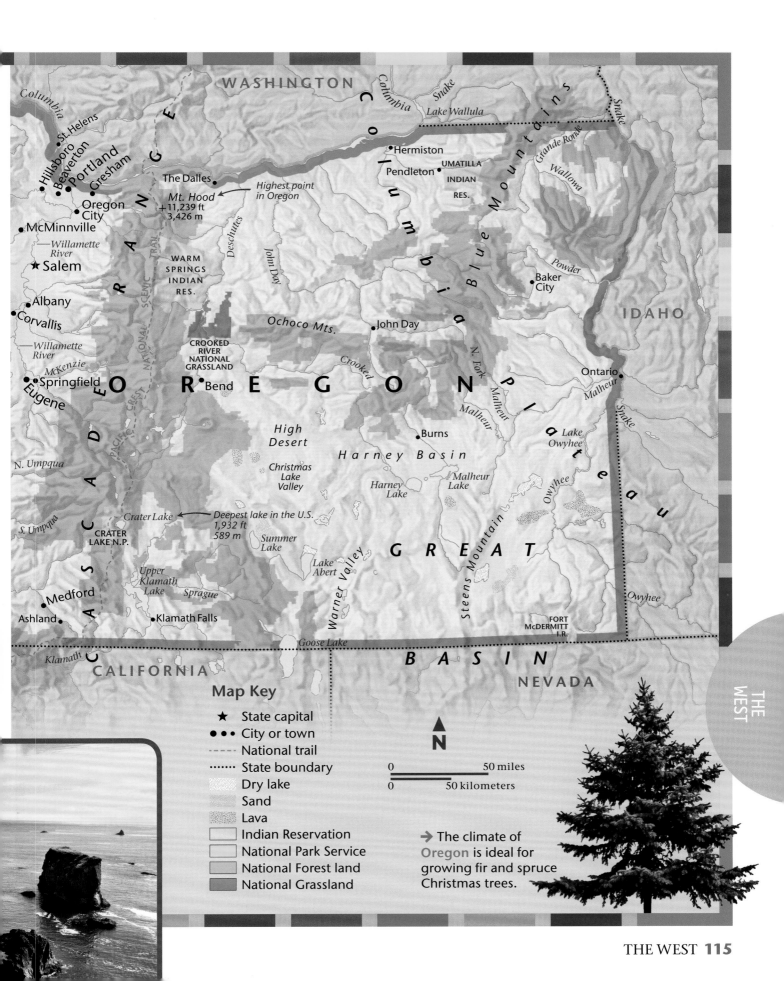

WASHINGTON

Columbia

Snake

Lake Wallula

Snake

Columbia

St. Helens
Hillsboro
Beaverton
Portland
Gresham

The Dalles

Hermiston

Pendleton

UMATILLA
INDIAN
RES.

Grande Ronde

Wallowa

Oregon
City

Mt. Hood
+11,239 ft
3,426 m

Highest point
in Oregon

Blue Mountains

McMinnville

*Willamette
River*

★ Salem

WARM
SPRINGS
INDIAN
RES.

Deschutes

John Day

Powder

Baker
City

Albany

Corvallis

*Willamette
River*

McKenzie

Springfield

Eugene

C A S C A D E O R A N G E

PACIFIC CREST NATIONAL SCENIC TRAIL

CROOKED
RIVER
NATIONAL
GRASSLAND

Bend

Ochoco Mts.

Crooked

John Day

O R E G O N   P l a t e a u

N. Fork

Malheur

Malheur

Ontario

Malheur

IDAHO

N. Umpqua

High
Desert

Christmas
Lake
Valley

Burns

Harney Basin

Malheur

Lake
Owyhee

Snake

S. Umpqua

Crater Lake

Deepest lake in the U.S.
1,932 ft
589 m

CRATER
LAKE N.P.

Summer
Lake

Harney
Lake

Malheur
Lake

Owyhee

Steens Mountain

G R E A T

Medford

Upper
Klamath
Lake

Sprague

Lake
Abert

Warner Valley

Ashland

Klamath Falls

FORT
McDERMITT
I.R.

Owyhee

Klamath

Goose Lake

B A S I N

CALIFORNIA

NEVADA

Map Key

★ State capital
••• City or town
---- National trail
······ State boundary
Dry lake
Sand
Lava
Indian Reservation
National Park Service
National Forest land
National Grassland

N

| 0 | | 50 miles |
| 0 | | 50 kilometers |

→ The climate of
Oregon is ideal for
growing fir and spruce
Christmas trees.

UTAH

Utah

↑ Water sports such as inner tubing are popular activities in **Glen Canyon National Recreation Area.**

Land & Water
The Great Basin, the Uinta Mountains, and Great Salt Lake are important land and water features of Utah.

Statehood
Utah became the 45th state in 1896.

People & Places
Utah's population is 2,995,919. Salt Lake City is the state capital and the largest city.

Fun Fact
Great Salt Lake is the largest natural lake west of the Mississippi River. The lake, which has a high level of evaporation, is about eight times saltier than the ocean.

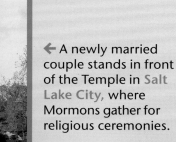

← A newly married couple stands in front of the Temple in **Salt Lake City,** where Mormons gather for religious ceremonies.

↓ Delicate Arch in **Arches National Park** is one of more than 2,000 arches that have been carved by natural forces over millions of years. The snowcapped La Sal Mountains stand in the distance.

Utah State Flag

Sego Lilly
State Flower

California Gull
State Bird

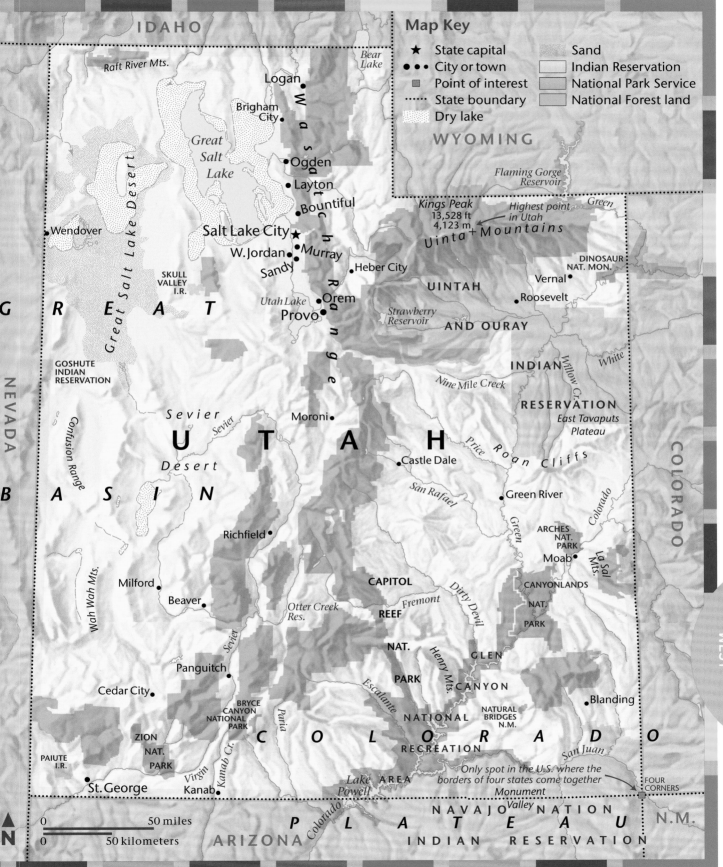

IDAHO

Raft River Mts.

Bear Lake

Logan

Brigham City

Great Salt Lake

Wendover

Great Salt Lake Desert

Ogden

Layton

Bountiful

Salt Lake City ★

W. Jordan

Murray

Sandy

Utah Lake

Orem

Provo

SKULL VALLEY I.R.

GOSHUTE INDIAN RESERVATION

Heber City

Sevier

Confusion Range

UTAH

Sevier Desert

Moroni

Castle Dale

Richfield

Milford

Beaver

Otter Creek Res.

Wah Wah Mts.

Panguitch

Cedar City

BRYCE CANYON NATIONAL PARK

ZION NAT. PARK

PAIUTE I.R.

St. George

Kanab

Paria

Kanab Cr.

Virgin

ARIZONA

COLORADO

Escalante

Lake Powell

Colorado

CAPITOL

REEF

NAT.

PARK

Fremont

Dirty Devil

Henry Mts.

GLEN

CANYON

NATURAL BRIDGES N.M.

NATIONAL

RECREATION

AREA

Only spot in the U.S. where the borders of four states come together

FOUR CORNERS

Monument Valley

NAVAJO NATION

INDIAN RESERVATION

PLATEAU

N.M.

★ State capital
••• City or town
▪ Point of interest
······ State boundary
Dry lake

Sand
Indian Reservation
National Park Service
National Forest land

WYOMING

Flaming Gorge Reservoir

Kings Peak 13,528 ft 4,123 m

Highest point in Utah

Uinta Mountains

Green

DINOSAUR NAT. MON.

UINTAH

Vernal

Roosevelt

Strawberry Reservoir

AND OURAY

White

Willow Creek

INDIAN

Nine Mile Creek

RESERVATION

East Tavaputs Plateau

Price

Roan Cliffs

San Rafael

Green River

Green

Colorado

ARCHES NAT. PARK

Moab

La Sal Mts.

CANYONLANDS

NAT.

PARK

Blanding

San Juan

COLORADO

NEVADA

GREAT

BASIN

G

NEVADA

COLORADO

THE WEST

0   50 miles
0   50 kilometers

N

THE WEST **117**

Washington

Land & Water
The Olympic Mountains, the Palouse Hills, and Puget Sound are important land and water features of Washington.

Statehood
Washington became the 42nd state in 1889.

People & Places
Washington's population is 7,170,351. Olympia is the state capital. The largest city is Seattle.

Fun Fact
Mount Rainier, a dormant volcano, last erupted in 1969. Another nearby volcano, Mount St. Helens, erupted in 1980. Winds carried ash from the eruption as far away as Maine.

↑ A Roosevelt elk grazes in the temperate rain forest of **Olympic National Forest**. Adult males weigh up to 1,000 pounds (454 kg).

← The modern skyline of **Seattle** is easily recognized because of its Space Needle tower. The city is an important West Coast port.

Washington State Flag

Coast Rhododendron
State Flower

American Goldfinch
State Bird

Strait
Vancouver Island
Cape Flattery
Strait of Juan de Fuca
MAKAH I.R.
Port Angeles
OLYMPIC N.F.
Olympic
OLYMPIC NAT. PARK
Mountains
QUINAULT INDIAN RES.
PACIFIC OCEAN
Grays Harbor
Willapa Bay
Cape Disappointment
COAST RANGES
Columbia

| 0 | 50 miles |
| 0 | 50 kilometers |

Map Key
★ State capital
●●● City or town
----- National trail
...... State boundary
••••• Country boundary
Glacier
Indian Reservation
National Park Service
National Forest land

CANADA
U.S.

CANADA
U.S.

Strait of Georgia

LUMMI
I.R.
● Bellingham

*San Juan
Islands*

NORTH
CASCADES

Ross Lake

ROSS LAKE
N.R.A.

RANGE

NATIONAL

Skagit

**Mount
Vernon**

*Whidbey
Island*

Oak Harbor

TULALIP
I.R.

Port
Townsend

OLYMPIC
NAT.
FOREST

● **Everett**

Skykomish

Kirkland ●

Redmond

Bremerton

Puget Sound

● Seattle
Bellevue
Renton

Auburn

Tacoma ●
Puyallup ●

★ Olympia

PUYALLUP I.R.

PARK

NATIONAL SCENIC TRAIL

*Lake
Chelan*

LAKE CHELAN
N.R.A.

Omak ●

Republic ●

Okanogan

Sanpoil

Colville ●

Columbia

RECREATION

NATIONAL

Franklin
Delano
Roosevelt
Lake

Colville

KALISPELL
I.R.

Pend

Oreille

COLVILLE
INDIAN
RESERVATION

LAKE   ROOSEVELT

SPOKANE
INDIAN
RES.

Spokane

Spokane ●

Spokane Valley

W A S H I N G T O N

Columbia

Grand Coulee

*Banks
Lake*

Ephrata ●

Moses Lake ●

Palouse

Wenatchee ●

Yakima

CASCADE

PACIFIC

CREST

Columbia

Ellensburg ●

*Potholes
Reservoir*

Hills

Pullman ●

*Mt. Rainier
14,411 ft
4,392 m* +

MT. RAINIER
N.P.

← *Highest
point in
Washington*

Chehalis

Chehalis ●

Yakima ●

Cowlitz

Toppenish ●

YAKAMA
INDIAN
RESERVATION

Yakima

Snake

*Lake
Sacajawea*

Pomeroy ●

Mount
St. Helens +

Chehalis

Longview ●

Vancouver ●

Goldendale ●

Prosser ●

Richland ●

Kennewick

Pasco ●

Lake Wallula

Walla Walla ●

Blue Mountains

Snake

Columbia

Plateau

IDAHO

O R E G O N

N

THE
WEST

← Tulips are big
business in the
Skagit River Valley,
where thousands
of these colorful
flowers bloom
every spring.

↑ An orca swims near the **San Juan Islands**. Also known
as killer whales, orcas live in groups called pods.

WYOMING

Wyoming

Land & Water
The Rocky Mountains, Yellowstone National Park, and the Green River are important land and water features of Wyoming.

Statehood
Wyoming became the 44th state in 1890.

People & Places
Wyoming's population is 586,107. Cheyenne is the state capital and the largest city.

Fun Fact
Wyoming is called the Equality State because it was the first state to give women the right to vote, granted in 1869 when it was still a territory.

↑ Steam and water from Old Faithful Geyser in **Yellowstone National Park** erupt more than 100 feet (30 m) into the air.

Map Key

★ State capital
•• City or town
⊐⊏ Pass
■ Point of interest
······ State Boundary
······ Continental Divide
☐ Indian Reservation
☐ National Park Service
☐ National Forest land
☐ National Grassland

Wyoming State Flag

Indian Paintbrush
State Flower

Western Meadowlark
State Bird

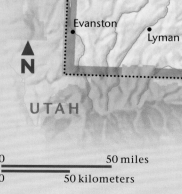

World's first national park, 1872

Yellowstone Lamar

YELLOWSTONE
Yellowstone Lake
OLD FAITHFUL
NAT. PARK

JOHN D. ROCKEFELLER, JR. MEM. PKWY.

Continental Divide

IDAHO

Snake

Teton Range

Jackson Lake

GRAND TETON NATIONAL PARK

• Jackson

Wyoming Range

Bear

Green

Fontenelle Reservoir

FOSSIL BUTTE NAT. MON.

Kemmerer • Hams Fork

• Evanston

• Lyman

N

UTAH

0   50 miles
0   50 kilometers

← The Wyoming state capitol building in **Cheyenne** was completed in 1890. It is now a U.S. national historic landmark.

MONTANA

SOUTH DAKOTA

BIGHORN CANYON N.R.A.

Lovell
Bighorn Lake
Shoshone
Cody
Buffalo Bill Reservoir
Greybull
Bighorn
Nowood
Sheridan
Clear Creek
Powder
Little Powder
THUNDER
Keyhole Reservoir
Sundance
Gillette
Belle Fourche
BASIN
Newcastle
Black Hills
Worland

Absaroka Range
Yellowstone
Wind
Highest point in Wyoming
Owl Creek
Thermopolis
Middle Fork
S. Fork Powder
Wright
NATIONAL
Cheyenne

WIND RIVER
Gannett Peak
13,804 ft
4,207 m
INDIAN
Ocean Lake
Wind
Boysen Reservoir

W Y O M I N G

GRASSLAND

RESERVATION
Riverton

Casper
North Platte
Douglas
Niobrara

Sweetwater
Pathfinder Reservoir
Glendo Reservoir

South Pass
Continental Divide
Seminoe Reservoir
Guernsey
North Platte

Big Sandy
Great Divide Basin
Medicine Bow
Hanna
Laramie

Green
Blacks Fork
Green River
Rock Springs
Continental Divide
Rawlins
Saratoga
North Platte
Medicine Bow
Horse Creek
Laramie

Flaming Gorge Reservoir
Lodgepole Creek

Green
COLORADO
Mts.
Cheyenne ★

Wind River Range
MOUNTAINS
Front Range
GREAT PLAINS
NEBRASKA

← The snowcapped peaks of the **Teton Range**, one of the West's youngest ranges, rise high above a meadow where horses graze.

→ Unique to the western **Great Plains**, the pronghorn can sprint up to 60 miles an hour (97 km/h).

THE WEST

The Territories

ACROSS TWO SEAS

Listed below are the five largest* of the fourteen U.S. territories, along with their flags and key information. Two are in the Caribbean Sea; the other three are in the Pacific Ocean. Can you find the other nine U.S. territories on the map?

U.S. CARIBBEAN TERRITORIES

PUERTO RICO

Area: 3,508 sq mi (9,086 sq km)

Population: 3,598,357

Capital: San Juan

Languages: Spanish, English

U.S. VIRGIN ISLANDS

Area: 149 sq mi (386 sq km)

Population: 103,574

Capital: Charlotte Amalie

Languages: English, Spanish or Spanish Creole, French or French Creole

U.S. PACIFIC TERRITORIES

AMERICAN SAMOA

Area: 77 sq mi (199 sq km)

Population: 54,343

Capital: Pago Pago

Languages: Samoan, English

NORTHERN MARIANA ISLANDS

Area: 184 sq mi (477 sq km)

Population: 52,344

Capital: Capital Hill

Languages: Philippine languages, Chamorro, English

GUAM

Area: 217 sq mi (561 sq km)

Population: 161,785

Capital: Hagåtña (Agana)

Languages: English, Filipino, Chamorro

OTHER U.S. TERRITORIES

Baker Island, Howland Island, Jarvis Island, Johnston Atoll, Kingman Reef, Midway Islands, Navassa Island, Palmyra Atoll, Wake Island

*Close-up views of the five largest territories are highlighted in enlarged inset maps labeled with a letter. You can see where each territory is by looking for its corresponding letter on the main map.

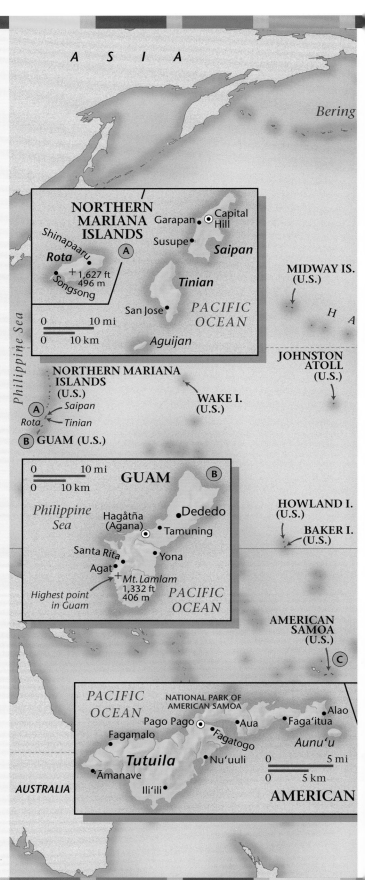

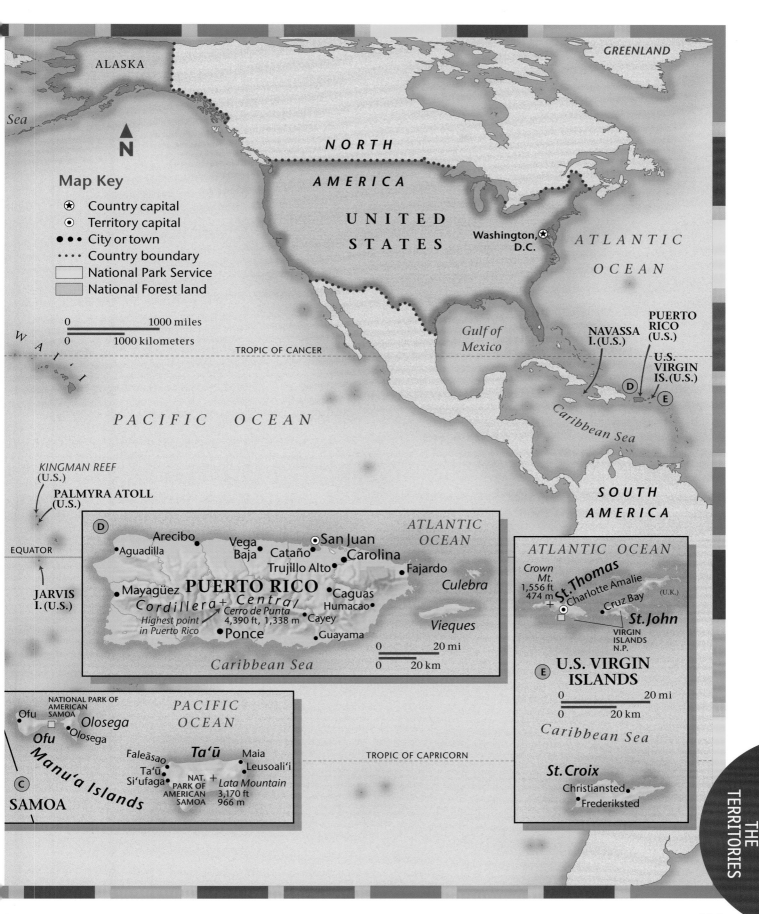

ALASKA

Sea

GREENLAND

N

Map Key

⍟ Country capital
⊙ Territory capital
●●● City or town
···· Country boundary
▭ National Park Service
▭ National Forest land

0 ——— 1000 miles
0 ——— 1000 kilometers

NORTH

AMERICA

UNITED

STATES

Washington, ⍟
D.C.

ATLANTIC

OCEAN

TROPIC OF CANCER

*Gulf of
Mexico*

NAVASSA
I.(U.S.)

PUERTO
RICO
(U.S.)

U.S.
VIRGIN
IS.(U.S.)

Ⓓ

Ⓔ

PACIFIC   OCEAN

Caribbean Sea

H
A
W
A
I
I

KINGMAN REEF
(U.S.)

PALMYRA ATOLL
(U.S.)

SOUTH

AMERICA

EQUATOR

**JARVIS
I.(U.S.)**

Puerto Rico inset (Ⓓ)

Ⓓ

ATLANTIC
OCEAN

Arecibo

Vega
Baja

Cataño

San Juan ⊙

Carolina

Aguadilla

Trujillo Alto

Fajardo

Culebra

Mayagüez

PUERTO RICO

Caguas

Humacao

Cordillera + Central
Cerro de Punta
Highest point → 4,390 ft, 1,338 m
in Puerto Rico

Cayey

Guayama

Vieques

Ponce

Caribbean Sea

0 ——— 20 mi
0 ——— 20 km

U.S. Virgin Islands inset (Ⓔ)

ATLANTIC   OCEAN

*Crown
Mt.
1,556 ft
474 m*
+

St.Thomas

Charlotte Amalie

(U.K.)

St.John

Cruz Bay

⊙

VIRGIN
ISLANDS
N.P.

Ⓔ **U.S. VIRGIN
ISLANDS**

0 ——— 20 mi
0 ——— 20 km

Caribbean Sea

St.Croix

Christiansted

Frederiksted

American Samoa inset (Ⓒ)

NATIONAL PARK OF
AMERICAN
SAMOA

Ofu

Olosega

Ofu

Olosega

PACIFIC
OCEAN

Faleāsao

Ta'ū

Maia

Ta'ū

Leusoali'i

Si'ufaga

NAT.
PARK OF
AMERICAN
SAMOA

+ *Lata Mountain*
3,170 ft
966 m

Manu'a Islands

Ⓒ

SAMOA

TROPIC OF CAPRICORN

The United States at a Glance

Land
Five Largest States by Area

1. **Alaska:** 663,267 sq mi (1,717,854 sq km)
2. **Texas:** 268,581 sq mi (695,624 sq km)
3. **California:** 163,696 sq mi (423,972 sq km)
4. **Montana:** 147,042 sq mi (380,840 sq km)
5. **New Mexico:** 121,590 sq mi (314,917 sq km)

Water
Primary Water Bodies Bordering the U.S.

1. **Pacific Ocean:** 65,436,200 sq mi (169,479,000 sq km)
2. **Atlantic Ocean:** 35,338,500 sq mi (91,526,400 sq km)
3. **Arctic Ocean:** 5,390,000 sq mi (13,960,100 sq km)
4. **Gulf of Mexico:** 591,430 sq mi (1,531,810 sq km)

Highest, Longest, Largest

The numbers below show locations on the map.

❶ **Highest Mountain**
Denali (Mount McKinley), in Alaska:
20,320 ft (6,194 m)

❷ **Longest River System**
Mississippi–Missouri: 3,710 mi (5,971 km)

❸ **Largest Freshwater Lake
(entirely in the U.S.)**
Lake Michigan:
22,300 sq mi (57,757 sq km)

❹ **Largest Saltwater Lake**
Great Salt Lake, in Utah:
1,700 sq mi (4,403 sq km)

❺ **Northernmost Point**
Point Barrow, Alaska

❻ **Southernmost Point**
Kalae, Hawai'i

❼ **Easternmost Point**
Sail Rock, West Quoddy Head, Maine

❽ **Westernmost Point**
Peaked Island, Alaska

People

In 2015 more than 320 million people live in the United States. Of these, more than 43 million were born in another country. The largest foreign-born group came from Mexico, followed by India, the Philippines, and China. By 2050 it is estimated that the country's population will approach 400 million, with 72 million being foreign-born.

Five Largest States by Number of People

1. **California:** 39,144,818 people
2. **Texas:** 27,469,114 people
3. **Florida:** 20,271,272 people
4. **New York:** 19,795,791 people
5. **Illinois:** 12,859,995 people

Five Largest Cities* by Number of People

1. **New York, NY:** 8,491,079 people
2. **Los Angeles, CA:** 3,928,864 people
3. **Chicago, IL:** 2,722,389 people
4. **Houston, TX:** 2,239,558 people
5. **Philadelphia, PA:** 1,560,297 people

*Figures are for city proper, not metropolitan area.

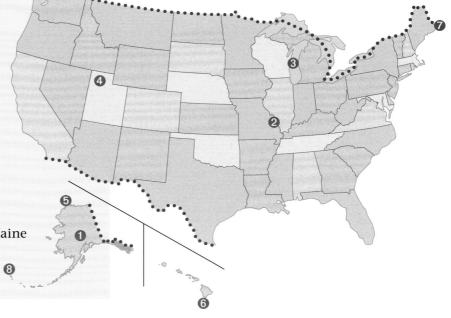

Glossary

Barrier island: a long sandy island that runs parallel to a shore

Bicentennial: the 200th anniversary of an event

Border State: during the Civil War, a slave state that stayed in the Union (Delaware, Kentucky, Maryland, and Missouri)

Boundary: an imaginary line that separates one political or mapped area from another; physical features (such as mountains and rivers) or latitude and longitude lines sometimes act as boundaries

Capital: a place where a country or state government is located

Coniferous forest: needleleaf trees that bear seeds in cones

Container ships: large ships that carry goods in truck-size metal containers among world ports

Contiguous U.S.: the 48 states that are joined together; excludes Alaska and Hawai'i

Continental U.S.: the 49 states located on the continent of North America; excludes Hawai'i

Continental Divide: a natural boundary line separating waters flowing into the Atlantic Ocean and Gulf of Mexico from those flowing into the Pacific Ocean

Creole: a blended language evolved from contact between two or more unrelated languages

Deciduous forests: trees, such as oak, maple, and beech, that lose their leaves in the cold season

Delmarva Peninsula: an East Coast peninsula named for the states it includes: Delaware, Maryland, and Virginia

Desert: a region with either hot or cold temperatures that receives ten inches (25 cm) or less of precipitation a year

Dormant volcano: a volcano that is currently inactive but that may erupt at some time in the future

Erosion: the process by which wind, water, or ice carries away rocks, soil, and other weathered material on Earth's surface

Estuary: the wide part of a river near a sea, where freshwater and saltwater mix

Exports: products made in one place and sent to another to be sold

Foothills: a region of lower hills at the base of a mountain

Fossil: an impression left by the remains of ancient animals or plants that has been preserved in rock or tree sap

Grassland: large areas of mainly flat land covered with grasses

High Plains: flat or gently rolling land above 2,000 feet (600 m); semiarid region east of the Rocky Mountains

Hydroelectric plant: a facility that uses the energy of moving water to create power

Indian reservation: land set aside by the U.S. government for Native Americans to live on and govern

Louisiana Purchase: land purchased from France in 1803 that stretched from the Mississippi River to the Rocky Mountains, and from the Gulf of Mexico to Canada, doubling the size of the country at that time

Mouth: place where a river empties into an ocean or other large body of water

Peninsula: a large piece of land that sticks out into the water

Petroleum: a type of fuel formed when the remains of marine plants and animals are buried beneath sediments and subjected to intense heat and pressure over millions of years

Sedimentary: a kind of rock, such as sandstone, made of small, compressed particles

Shakers: members of a religious group who did not marry and lived in communal societies

Sunbelt: a region of the southern and western U.S. experiencing rapid economic growth and major in-migration of population

Territory: land under the rule of a country but that is not a state or a province of that country

Temperate rain forest: forests found along the Pacific coast of North America where there is a cool, moist climate and where rainfall is abundant

Tropical rain forest: a region occurring mostly in a belt between the Tropic of Cancer and Tropic of Capricorn in areas that have at least 80 inches (200 cm) of rain each year and an average yearly temperature of 77°F (25°C)

Tundra: a region at high latitudes or high elevations that has cold temperatures, low vegetation, and a short growing season

Wetland: land that is covered with or soaked by water; includes swamps, marshes, and bogs

Index

Pictures and the text that describes them have their page numbers printed in **bold** type.

Two-Letter Postal Codes

Since 1888, the National Geographic Society has funded more than 12,000 research, exploration, and preservation projects around the world. The Society receives funds from National Geographic Partners, LLC, funded in part by your purchase. A portion of the proceeds from this book supports this vital work. To learn more, visit www.natgeo.com/info.

For more information, visit www.nationalgeographic.com, call 1-800-647-5463, or write to the following address:
National Geographic Partners, LLC
1145 17th Street N.W.
Washington, D.C. 20036-4688 U.S.A.

Visit us online at nationalgeographic.com/books

For librarians and teachers: ngchildrensbooks.org

More for kids from National Geographic: kids.nationalgeographic.com

For information about special discounts for bulk purchases, please contact National Geographic Books Special Sales: ngspecsales@ngs.org

For rights or permissions inquiries, please contact National Geographic Books Subsidiary Rights: ngbookrights@ngs.org

NATIONAL GEOGRAPHIC and Yellow Border Design are trademarks of the National Geographic Society, used under license.

Designed by Jim Hiscott, Jr.

Paperback ISBN: 978-1-4263-2647-9
Hardcover ISBN: 978-1-4263-2434-5
Reinforced library binding ISBN: 978-1-4263-2435-2

Printed in China
16/RRDS/2

Illustrations Credits

Front cover: (background), Brandon Laufenberg/Getty Images; (Sacagawea), Patrick Faricy; (George Washington), Everett Historical/Shutterstock; (boy on rope swing), Corbis; (U.S. globe), ymgerman/iStockphoto; (baseball), Dan Thornberg/Shutterstock; (Seattle Space Needle), Digital Stock; (Route 66 sign), Photodisc; (Lincoln Memorial), Alexander Shor/E+/Getty Images; (cherry pie), BRAND X; (bald eagle), EyeWire Images; (totem pole), Photodisc; (stamp outline), Neftali/Shutterstock; (stamp outline), stamp outline/Shutterstock; Spine: (Chrysler Building), Danita Delimont/Getty Images; Back cover: (riverboat), Photodisc; (lizard), MWaits/Shutterstock; (lake and mountain), Photodisc; (bald eagle flying), Sekar B/Shutterstock; (hot dog), mj007/Shutterstock

Front matter: 1 (background), Brandon Laufenberg/Getty Images; 1 (UP LE), zschnepf/Shutterstock; 1 (UP RT), Taylor Kennedy/National Geographic Creative; 1 (LO LE), Eric Isselée/Shutterstock; 1 (LO RT), John Kelly/Iconica/Getty Images; 1 (LO CTR), Paul Tillinghast/Getty Images; 2 (LE), Alaska Stock Images/NationalGeographicStock.com; 2 (RT), SergeyIT/Shutterstock; 2 (LO), Rob Byron/Shutterstock; 3 (UP LE), metalstock/Shutterstock; 3 (LO LE), Zuzule/Shutterstock; 3 (UP RT), Eric Isselée/Shutterstock; 3 (CTR), James M Phelps, Jr/Shutterstock; 3 (RT), Geoffrey Kuchera/Shutterstock; 6 (LO LE), erllre74/Shutterstock; 6 (UP RT), Charles Krebs/Riser/Getty Images; 6 (CTR RT), Mike Brake/Shutterstock; 6 (LO RT), James Randklev/Riser/Getty Images; 7, Olivier Le Queinec/Shutterstock; 8 (UP), Billy Hustace/Stone/Getty Images; 8 (LO), sonya etchison/Shutterstock; 9 (LE), Mark R/Shutterstock; 9 (RT), dibrova/Shutterstock; 10 (CTR), PhotoDisc; 10-11 (UP), PhotoDisc; 11 (UP RT), Taylor S. Kennedy/NationalGeographicStock.com; 11 (LO), Jahi Chikwendiu/The Washington Post/Getty Images; THE NORTHEAST: 12 (LO), Alaska Stock Images/NationalGeographicStock.com; 12-13, Skip Brown/NationalGeographicStock.com; 14 (UP), Shawn Pecor/Shutterstock; 14 (LO), Donald Gargano/Shutterstock; 15, Joel Sartore/NationalGeographicStock.com; 16 (CTR), Kevin Fleming/Corbis; 16-17 (UP), Jake Rajs/Stome/Getty Images; 16-17 (LO), William S. Kuta/Alamy; 17 (UP RT), Catherine Lane/iStockphoto.com; 18 (CTR), Mikael Damkier/Shutterstock; 18 (LO), Jeff Schultes/Shutterstock; 18-19 (UP), PhotoDisc; 19 (LO), Noah Strycker/Shutterstock; 20 (UP), Emory Kristof/NationalGeographicStock.com; 20 (LO), Jeremy Edwards/iStockphoto.com; 21 (UP), Justine Gecewicz/iStockphoto.com; 21 (LO), James L. Stanfield/NationalGeographicStock.com; 22 (UP), Christopher Penler/Shutterstock; 22 (LO), Lijuan Guo/Shutterstock; 23 (LE), Chee-Onn Leong/Shutterstock; 23 (RT), Brett Atkins/Shutterstock; 24 (UP), Paula Stephens/Shutterstock; 24 (CTR), Marcel Jancovic/Shutterstock; 24 (LO), George & Judy Manna/Photo Researchers RM/Getty Images; 25, Tony Campbell/Shutterstock; 26 (UP), Dave Raboin/iStockphoto.com; 26 (CTR), Steve Miller/The Star-Ledger/Corbis; 26-27 (LO), Aimin Tang/iStockphoto.com; 27 (UP), Sheldon Kralstein/iStockphoto.com; 27 (CTR), Andrew F. Kazmierski/Shutterstock; 28 (UP), Cathleen Abers-Kimball/iStockphoto.com; 28-29 (LO), Richard Levine/Alamy; 29 (RT), Glenn Taylor/iStockphoto.com; 30, iStockphoto.com; 31 (LE), Jeremy Edwards/iStockphoto.com; 31 (RT), Racheal Grazias/Shutterstock; 32 (CTR), Mona Makela/Shutterstock; 32 (LO), Joy Brown/Shutterstock; 32-33 (UP), Yare Marketing/Shutterstock; 33 (LO), Robert Kelsey/Shutterstock; 34 (UP), Thomas M Perkins/Shutterstock; 34 (LO), sianc/Shutterstock; 35 (UP), Parker Deen/iStockphoto.com; 35 (LO), rebvt/Shutterstock; THE SOUTHEAST: 36 (LO), SergeyIT/Shutterstock; 36-37, Maria Stenzel/NationalGeographicStock.com; 38 (UP), Darryl Vest/Shutterstock; 38 (CTR), Kevin Fleming/Corbis; 38-39 (LO), Wayne James/Shutterstock; 39 (CTR), Ronnie Howard/Shutterstock; 40 (UP), courtesy of the Museum of Discovery, www.museumofdiscovery.org; 40 (LO), Bill Barksdale/Corbis; 41, Travel Bug/Shutterstock; 42 (UP), Wayne Johnson/iStockphoto.com; 42 (LO), NASA; 43 (UP), Varina and Jay Patel/iStockphoto.com; 43 (LO), Valentyn Volkov/Shutterstock; 44 (UP), jackweichen_gatech/Shutterstock; 44 (CTR), Antonio V. Oquias/Shutterstock; 44 (LO), Brian Lasenby/Shutterstock; 45, Andrew F. Kazmierski/Shutterstock; 46 (UP), Leon Ritter/Shutterstock; 46 (CTR), Craig Wactor/Shutterstock; 46 (LO), Anne Kitzman/Shutterstock; 47, Neale Cousland/Shutterstock; 48 (UP), Bob Sacha/Corbis; 48 (CTR), Jim Richardson/Corbis; 48 (LO), J. Helgason/Shutterstock; 49 (LE), Stephen Helstowski/Shutterstock; 49 (RT), Kathryn Bell/Shutterstock; 50 (UP), Vilmos Varga/Shutterstock; 50 (CTR), Daniela Duncan/Getty Images; 50 (LO), Peter Arnold, Inc./Alamy; 51, Mike Flippo/Shutterstock; 52 (LE), Leah-Anne Thompson/Shutterstock; 52 (RT), Forrest L. Smith, III/Shutterstock; 53 (LE), Rob Byron/Shutterstock; 53 (RT), Brad Whitsitt/Shutterstock; 54, Rafael Ramirez Lee/Shutterstock; 55 (UP), Richard Ellis/Getty Images; 55 (LO), Zach Holmes/Alamy; 56 (UP), Envision/Corbis; 56 (LO), Bryan Busovicki/Shutterstock; 57 (LE), Wayne James/Shutterstock; 57 (RT), Jennifer King/Shutterstock; 58 (UP), Darren K. Fisher/Shutterstock; 58 (LO), Travel Bug/Shutterstock; 59 (LE), graham s. klotz/Shutterstock; 59 (RT), Adam Bies/Shutterstock; 60 (CTR), Ken Inness/Shutterstock; 60 (LO), Mary Terriberry/Shutterstock; 60-61 (UP), Robert Pernell/Shutterstock; 61 (RT), Adam Bies/Shutterstock; THE MIDWEST: 62 (LO), metalstock/Shutterstock; 62-63, Jim Brandenburg/Minden Pictures; 64 (UP), Ralf-Finn Hestoft/Corbis; 64 (CTR), Tim Boyle/Getty Images; 64 (LO), Jenny Solomon/Shutterstock; 65, Kim Karpeles/Alamy; 66 (UP), James Steidl/Shutterstock; 66 (UP), Todd Taulman/Shutterstock; 66 (CTR), john j. klaiber jr/Shutterstock; 66-67 (LO), Melissa Farlow/NationalGeographicStock.com; 68 (UP), jokter/Shutterstock; 68 (LO), Madeleine Openshaw/Shutterstock; 69 (LE), steve schneider/iStockphoto.com; 69 (RT), Andre Jenny/Alamy; 70 (UP), aceshot1/Shutterstock; 70 (LO), Rusty Dodson/Shutterstock; 71, Bruce Dale/NationalGeographicStock.com; 72 (UP), Gary Paul Lewis/Shutterstock; 72 (CTR), Rachel L. Sellers/Shutterstock; 72 (LO), John Brueske/Shutterstock; 73, Cornelia Schaible/iStockphoto.com; 74 (UP), Maxim Kulko/Shutterstock; 74 (CTR), V. J. Matthew/Shutterstock; 74 (LO), Geoffrey Kuchera/Shutterstock; 75, Karla Caspari/Shutterstock; 76 (UP), Neil Phillip Mey/Shutterstock; 76 (LO), Jose Gil/Shutterstock; 77 (LE), Tim Pleasant/Shutterstock; 77 (RT), Rusty Dodson/Shutterstock; 78 (UP), Bates Littlehales/NationalGeographicStock.com; 78-79 (LO), James L. Amos/NationalGeographicStock.com; 79 (UP), Joel Sartore/NationalGeographicStock.com; 79 (LO RT), Jim Richardson/NationalGeographicStock.com; 80 (UP), Ian Martin/NationalGeographicStock.com; 80 (CTR), Randy Olson/NationalGeographicStock.com; 80 (LO), Rusty Dodson/Shutterstock; 81, iofoto/Shutterstock; 82 (UP), aceshot1/Shutterstock; 82 (CTR), Alex Neauville/Shutterstock; 82 (LO), James M Phelps, Jr/Shutterstock; 83, Weldon Schloneger/Shutterstock; 84 (UP), Werner Bollmann/Photolibrary/Getty Images; 84 (CTR), Ira Block/NationalGeographicStock.com; 84 (LO), iofoto/Shutterstock; 85, Danita Delimont/Alamy; 86 (UP LE), Aga/Shutterstock; 86 (UP RT), Brad Thompson/Shutterstock; 86 (CTR), Volkman K. Wentzel/NationalGeographicStock.com; 86 (LO), Alvis Upitis/AgStock Images/Corbis; 87, Layne Kennedy/Corbis; THE SOUTHWEST: 88 (LO), Zuzule/Shutterstock; 88-89, Jack Dykinga/NationalGeographicStock.com; 90 (UP), Michael Nichols/NationalGeographicStock.com; 90 (CTR), Zschnepf/Shutterstock; 90 (LO), Chris Curtis/Shutterstock; 92 (UP), italianestro/Shutterstock; 92 (CTR), Mariusz S. Jurgielewicz/Shutterstock; 92 (LO), Ralph Lee Hopkins/NationalGeographicStock.com; 94 (UP), Clint Spencer/iStockphoto.com; 94 (LO), Phil Anthony/Shutterstock; 95 (LE), Lindsay Hebberd/Corbis; 95 (RT), MWaits/Shutterstock; 96 (UP), Ben Conlan/iStockphoto.com; 96 (CTR), Mira/Alamy; 96 (LO), Rusty Dodson/Shutterstock; 97, B. Anthony Stewart/NationalGeographicStock.com; THE WEST: 98 (LO), Eric Isselée/Shutterstock; 98-99, Gordon Wiltsie/NationalGeographicStock.com; 100 (UP), Benoit Rousseau/iStockphoto.com; 100 (LO), alysta/Shutterstock; 101, Michael Pemberton/Shutterstock; 102 (UP), Stas Volik/Shutterstock; 102 (CTR), Bates Littlehales/NationalGeographicStock.com; 102 (LO), Lindsay Noechel/Shutterstock; 103, Elke Dennis/Shutterstock; 104 (UP), Larsek/Shutterstock; 104 (LO), PhotoDisc; 105, John Kelly/Iconica/Getty Images; 106 (CTR), Jim Sugar/Corbis; 106 (LO), Alex Staroseltsev/Shutterstock; 106-107 (UP), jarvis gray/Shutterstock; 107 (UP RT), Steve Raymer/NationalGeographicStock.com; 107 (CTR RT), Jeff Hunter/Photographer's Choice/Getty Images; 108 (UP), Bryan Brazil/Shutterstock; 108 (CTR), Raymond Gehman/NationalGeographicStock.com; 108 (LO), David P. Smith/Shutterstock; 109, Dick Durrance II/NationalGeographicStock.com; 110 (UP), Noah Clayton/The Image Bank/Getty Images; 110 (LO), Doug Lemke/Shutterstock; 111 (LE), Geoffrey Kuchera/Shutterstock; 111 (RT), Jerry Sharp/Shutterstock; 112 (CTR), W. Robert Moore/NationalGeographicStock.com; 112 (LO), Sam Abell/NationalGeographicStock.com; 112-113 (UP), Andy Z./Shutterstock; 113, Danita Delimont/Alamy; 114 (UP), Jennifer Lynn Arnold/Shutterstock; 114 (CTR), Rachell Coe/Shutterstock; 114-115 (LO), Peter Kunasz/Shutterstock; 115 (RT), Tischenko Irina/Shutterstock; 116 (UP), Grafton Marshall Smith/Corbis; 116 (CTR), Nelson Sirlin/Shutterstock; 116 (LO), PhotoDisc; 118 (UP), Natalia Bratslavsky/Shutterstock; 118 (LO), Luis Salazar/Shutterstock; 119 (LE), oksana.perkins/Shutterstock; 119 (RT), Sandy Buckley/Shutterstock; 120 (UP), Videowokart/Shutterstock; 120 (LO), Henryk Sadura/Shutterstock; 121 (LE), Peter Kunasz/Shutterstock; 121 (RT), Nancy Bauer/Shutterstock